MAY 1 5 2014

DAT

Bloom's Modern Critical Views

Bloom's Modern Critical Views

JACK LONDON

Edited and with an introduction by
Harold Bloom
Sterling Professor of the Humanities
Yale University

BLOOM'S
LITERARY CRITICISM
An imprint of Infobase Publishing

813.52
Bloom

Bloom's Literary Criticism
An imprint of Infobase Learning
132 West 31st Street
New York NY 10001

Library of Congress Cataloging-in-Publication Data
Jack London / edited and with an introduction by Harold Bloom. — New ed.
     p. cm. — (Bloom's modern critical views)
   Includes bibliographical references and index.
   ISBN 978-1-60413-366-0 (hardcover)
   1. London, Jack, 1876–1916—Criticism and interpretation.   I. Bloom, Harold.
   PS3523.O46Z649 2011
   813'.52—dc22
                                        2010036210

Bloom's Literary Criticism books are available at special discounts when purchased in bulk quantities for businesses, associations, institutions, or sales promotions. Please call our Special Sales Department in New York at (212) 967-8800 or (800) 322-8755.

You can find Bloom's Literary Criticism on the World Wide Web at
http://www.chelseahouse.com

Contributing editor: Pamela Loos
Cover designed by Takeshi Takahashi
Composition by IBT Global, Troy NY
Cover printed by IBT Global, Troy NY
Book printed and bound by IBT Global, Troy NY
Date printed: January 2011
Printed in the United States of America

10 9 8 7 6 5 4 3 2 1

This book is printed on acid-free paper.

All links and Web addresses were checked and verified to be correct at the time of publication. Because of the dynamic nature of the Web, some addresses and links may have changed since publication and may no longer be valid.

Contents

Editor's Note

My introduction grapples with London as writer and mythic figure in accounting for his continuing appeal. Donald Pizer similarly strives to uncover the source of London's canonical endurance given the superficiality of much of his work. Sam S. Baskett then pores over the author's letters in his reassessment of London's intentions in *The Sea-Wolf*.

Jonathan Auerbach explores the narrative self-consciousness afforded the various animal protagonists found in the novels, followed by Andrew J. Furer's assessment of the role of race.

Christopher Gair then suggests that the telegraph and developing communications technology deeply affected journalistic and literary style in early twentieth century. James A. Papa Jr. similarly appraises *The Sea-Wolf* through the lens of the period's historical and, specifically, nautical changes.

Per Serritslev Petersen traces London's quest to fuse fictional with philosophical authenticity, followed by Lisa Hopkins who joins the growing number of critics scrutinizing evolution and eugenics in the major writings. Lawrence I. Berkove concludes the volume by also taking up the evolutionary call, suggesting that London's greatest influence was Darwin.

HAROLD BLOOM

Introduction

Jack London died at 40 in 1916, possibly of a drug overdose. As autodidact, the self-named Jack London worked as an oyster pirate, a seaman, and a power plant laborer but was most himself as a vagrant and a revolutionary, until he became a professional writer and then a war correspondent. A voyager, rancher, socialist politician, a permanent adventurer, an incessant writer: London's energies were beyond measure. He remains both a phenomenon of our imaginative literature and a permanent figure in the American mythology.

His best stories—including "To Build a Fire," "The She-Wolf," "For the Love of a Man," and "The Apostate"—surpass his novels and fantasies in literary power. The realism of the stories is so extreme and intense that they border on hallucinatory phantasmagorias. Dogs transmute into wolves, if they are not eaten by wolves, and men struggle lest they themselves are devoured. Death is everywhere in Jack London's Klondike: freezing, starvation, and wolves fuse into a composite menace.

The Call of the Wild opens with a section called "Into the Primitive," which is a fair motto for Jack London's literary quest. Here I want to center on "The She-Wolf," the second story or episode of *White Fang*. London's grim sense of determinism haunts the entire book, whose opening section, "The Trail of the Meat," sums up the metaphysic of the work:

> It is not the way of the Wild to like movement. Life is an offense to it, for life is movement; and the Wild aims always to destroy movement. It freezes the water to prevent it running to the sea; it

1

drives the sap out of the trees till they are frozen in their mighty hearts; and most ferociously and terribly of all does the Wild harry and crush into submission man—man, who is the most restless of life, ever in revolt against the dictum that all movement must in the end come to the cessation of movement.

Jack London writes in the interval between Schopenhauer's analysis of the will to live and Freud's uncanny apprehension that the inanimate is our destination and origin, the vision of *Beyond the Pleasure Principle.* Yet London, though he gives the "Wild" his allegiance, retains a kind of last-ditch humanism. Bill and Henry, hunted by the wolf pack, "two men who are not yet dead," are marked by the dignity of their mutual regard and their desperate courage. Down to three bullets and six sled dogs, they are vastly outnumbered by the wolves. Their particular nemesis is the she-wolf, a husky sled dog gone back to the wild and now a leader of the wolf pack.

In the next episode, Bill joins the dogs as the she-wolf's victim, and Henry is a solitary survivor. It is London's peculiar power that his empathy extends equally to the she-wolf and to her human antagonists. Among writers of children's literature, London's stance would be more commonplace. I cannot think of a full analogue, in adult popular literature, to London's affinity for animals, except for Kipling, who so beautifully blurs the line between the child's and the adult's imagination. Kipling was a far more versatile and gifted writer than Jack London and had nothing in him of London's savage primitivism. But that worship of the wild still marks London's difference from nearly everyone else and accounts for London's permanent appeal to readers throughout the world.

DONALD PIZER

Jack London: The Problem of Form

Most of the significant criticism of Jack London has been devoted to two interrelated issues: Is there a coherent center to London's ideas or are they indeed hopelessly confused and contradictory; and what are the sources of London's strength and appeal as a writer given the superficiality of much of his work? So, for example, critics have often grappled with the relationship between London's socialism and Nietzscheanism, and they have sought to explain how a writer who could achieve the seamless perfection of "To Build a Fire" could also produce an extraordinary amount of trash. Whatever the value of these efforts, almost all have been piecemeal in character. The critic tackles a particular narrow problem or a specific work and then extrapolates from it. At the considerable risk of moving to the other extreme of overschematization and overgeneralization, I would like to suggest a single dominant solution to the enigma which is Jack London. The notion which I propose to pursue is that London as a thinker and as an artist is essentially a writer of fables and parables.

To help clear the ground, I should note that I do not maintain that there is a clear distinction between the fable and the parable.[1] Both forms are didactic. They seek to establish the validity of a particular moral truth by offering a brief story in which plot, character, and setting are allegorical agents of a paraphrasable moral. But historically, because of the association of

From *Studies in the Literary Imagination* 16, no. 2 (Fall 1983): 107–15. Copyright © 1983 by Georgia State University.

fable with Aesop and of parable with the Bible, each of the terms also has a more specialized coloration. By fable is usually meant a work in which beasts (and occasionally inanimate objects) both speak and represent human qualities, and by parable is meant a work in which the principal agents are human. Furthermore, the moral of a fable is apt to be far more worldly than that of a parable. Fables deal with how men act on earth, parables with how they should act to gain salvation.

Fables and parables are not fiction in our modern sense of the distinctive nature of fiction. They simplify experience into useable precept rather than render it as either complex or ambivalent. But in that simplification lies a potential for artistic strength if artistry in this instance can be said to be the restatement in pleasing form of what we as a race or society wish to hear about ourselves. The special appeal of the beast fable is that it substitutes wit for insight; it expresses not deep or fresh perception but rather a concise and clever recapitulation of what everybody knows. In the beast fable foxes are always shrewd, lions bold, hawks predatory, sheep silly, asses stupid, and so on. Setting is nonexistent or minimal and when present is a condition of the moral dilemma in which the beasts find themselves (a forest is danger, a barn safety). And action is limited to that which renders immediately and clearly the heart of the precept.

Much of the attraction of the fable lies not only in our pleasure in finding clearly recognizable human characteristics confirmed in animals but in the nature of the precepts which these characteristics advance. For the wisdom of the fable is the ancient wisdom of the world—that the shrewd and strong prevail unless blinded by pride, that greed is a great equalizer, and so on. The lesson of the fable is that the world is a place of seeking and grasping in which specific qualities of human nature always receive their just dessert. In the fable, vanity is always victimized by shrewdness, disappointment always seeks rationalization, and desire for gain guides all life.

Parable often moves beyond the way we are to the way we should be. While the precept of a fable is both concrete and expedient (be less vain and you shall prosper more), that of a parable tends toward moral abstractions (be charitable and you will be a better person). And since the ability to frame and respond to moral abstractions is a distinctively human attribute, the personae in a parable are almost always human.

By the late nineteenth century, whatever lines of demarcation that might have existed earlier between fable and parable had for the most part disappeared. In Kipling's *The Jungle Book*, for example, the worldliness of the beast fable and the more programmatic moralism of the parable join in clear allegories containing both animal and human characters. It was to this blending of the fable/parable form that London was powerfully drawn.

It seems strange today that the principal critical issue for many early readers of the most obviously fabulistic of London's fiction, his dog stories, was their problematical accuracy in depicting the conditions of natural life. After the great success of *The Call of the Wild* and *White Fang* (as well as the contemporary popularity of other nature fiction), Theodore Roosevelt, in a famous controversy of 1907, attacked London (among others) as a "nature faker." Referring to the fight between a lynx and a wolf in *White Fang*, Roosevelt commented, "Nobody who really knew anything about either a lynx or a wolf would write such nonsense." He then went on to reveal his misunderstanding of the form in which London was writing. "If the stories of these writers were written in the spirit that inspired Mowgli [the human figure in Kipling's *The Jungle Book*], . . . we should be content to read, enjoy, and accept them as fables. . . . But when such fables are written by a make-believe realist, the matter assumes an entirely different complexion."[2]

Of course, criticism of London has advanced far beyond Roosevelt's demand that animal fiction should announce itself clearly as either fabulistic or realistic. For example, in a striking reading of *The Call of the Wild* and *White Fang*, Earle Labor has suggested that the permanent appeal of these works is that they are beast fables whose endorsement of the myth of the hero and of the value of primordial strength rings true in our collective unconscious.[3] Labor's Jungian reading of these works is the most useful which has yet appeared, but I believe that a more immediate reason for the appeal and holding power of London's best work lies in their form.

London's work falls roughly into three groups related to his "natural" inclination to work in the fable/parable form. The first, which includes *The Call of the Wild* and *White Fang* as well as such stories as "To Build a Fire" and "The Chinago," reveals his ability to rely unconsciously yet with great success on the underlying characteristics of the fable/parable. The second, which includes *The Iron Heel* and such stories as "The Apostate" and "The Strength of the Strong," suggests that when London wrote consciously in the parable form—as he did in these works—he sacrificed power for ideological obviousness. And the third, which includes a large number of London's novels and short stories, but most significantly *The Sea-Wolf*, indicates that London's efforts to write conventional fiction were usually handicapped by his inadequacies in this form, but that such works are occasionally rescued by their fabulistic element. Finally, I will also suggest that much that is distinctive and valuable in London's autobiographical writing—in *The Road*, *Martin Eden*, and *John Barleycorn*—can be viewed as an extension into this form of his penchant for the fable/parable.

I

The Call of the Wild and *White Fang* are companion allegories of the response of human nature to heredity and environment. Both Buck and White Fang begin their lives with a mixture of the primitive and the civilized in their condition. Buck is raised in the Southland (London's allegorical setting for civilization), but, like all dogs, has an atavistic strain of wolf in his make-up. White Fang, though largely wolf and though bred in the Far North, contains an element of the civilized through his part-dog mother. The novels demonstrate the effects of a change in environment on the two dogs. Buck, abducted into a Northland world of the ruthless struggle for existence, calls forth from his racial past the strength and cunning necessary to survive in this world, and eventually becomes the leader of a wolf-pack in a people-less wilderness. White Fang is drawn into civilization, first by Indians, then by miners, and finally, in the Southland, by upper middle class ranchers, and becomes doglike in his loyalty and love toward his master.

What appeals in the two works is not London's dramatization of a particular late nineteenth-century Darwinian formulation but rather his powerful use of the principal ethical thrust and formal characteristics of the fable, with an admixture as well of the parable. Characterization is at a minimum in the two works; dogs and men are types and the types themselves are moral in nature. In *Call*, Charles, Hal, and Mercedes (the three "tenderfoot" Klondikers who buy Buck) are Vanity and Ignorance, and John Thornton is Loyalty and Love. The dogs in the story are even more clearly moral types—Laziness, Envy, Fear, Honesty, and so on. In *White Fang*, Kiche is the Mother, Beauty Smith (who exhibits White Fang) is Evil, and Weedon Scott is Thornton's counterpart. Setting is allegorical in both works, with London exaggerating for symbolic clarity both the "softness" of the South and the competitive animality of the North. And action is symbolic within the clear lines of thematic movement of Buck's return to the primitive and White Fang's engagement by civilization. Perhaps most important of all, theme itself is essentially proverbial rather than ideological. It is not so much Darwin and Spencer who supply the thematic core of the two novels as Aesop and the Bible. For *Call of the Wild* proposes the wisdom of the beast fable that the strong, the shrewd, and the cunning shall prevail when, as is progressively true in this story, life is bestial. And *White Fang* endorses the Christian wisdom that all shall lie down together in peace when love predominates.

Both *Call* and *White Fang* contain—to a degree not usually sufficiently stressed—a strong element of the Christian parable within their beast fable emphasis on the competitive nature of experience. Buck's response to the kindness, justness, and warmth of Thornton is love; it is only with the death of Thornton that he becomes the Ghost Dog of the wilderness. And White

Fang, when rescued from the brutality of Beauty Smith by Weedon Scott and when "educated" in affection by Scott, also responds with love. The moral allegory is clear in both works. Man hovers between the primitive and the civilized both in his make-up and in his world, and it is his capacity for love which often determines which direction he will take. Again, this theme is not so much specifically ideological as it is racial wisdom, with that wisdom embodied in a form which makes it pleasingly evident.

An obvious question, given the similarities in theme and form between the two works, is why *The Call of the Wild* is generally held to be superior to *White Fang*. An answer lies, I believe, in the greater conformity of *Call* to the beast fable form in two significant areas. First, *White Fang* makes greater pretentions to the range and fullness of a novel. Fabulistic brevity and conciseness, and thus symbolic sharpness, are sacrificed for lengthy development of each phase of White Fang's career. And since we can anticipate from the beginning the nature and direction of his evolution, the doldrums occasionally set in. But also, as Earle Labor has pointed out, we are inherently more interested in an account of a return to the primitive than one of an advance into civilization. Labor suggests, as I noted earlier, that this difference in attraction lies in the greater appeal which *Call* makes to our unconscious longing for primitive simplicity and freedom. But this greater holding power may derive as well—and more immediately—from the fuller endorsement in *Call* of the Aesopian wisdom that the strong prevail. There is not much love in Aesop, but there is much demonstration that it is better to be powerful in a world in which power controls destiny.

London's best known and most admired story, "To Build a Fire," is also a fable/parable in the sense that I have discussed *The Call of the Wild* and *White Fang*. The story reveals London's ability to use the conventions of the form not only in works centering on animals but also in those in which human characters predominate. As in *Call* and *White Fang*, London in "To Build a Fire" (as well as in such a first-rate story as "The Chinago") involves us in a fable/parable without his conscious awareness that he is exploiting an allegory to deliver a message.[4] In "To Build a Fire," the *chechaquo*, or "newcomer in the land," is Ignorance, and the setting in which he finds himself, the extraordinary frost of a Yukon cold snap, is Danger. From its opening words, the fable moves toward its resolution of these two permanent conditions of life. As in London's dog stories, the moral of "To Build a Fire" rests more on racial wisdom than Darwinian ideology, just as in "The Chinago"—a story in which a Chinese coolie in Tahiti is wrongly executed for a murder—the fabulistic moral that men will destroy rather than acknowledge and rectify a mistake is more powerfully felt than any social protest theme arising out of the exploitation of coolie labor in the South Seas. In "To Build a Fire," the success of the story, as in the successful fable, stems from our acceptance of its worldly wisdom while simultaneously admiring the formal devices used to communicate it—in this instance, the ironic disparity between our knowledge of Danger and the newcomer's Ignorance of it, and the brevity and clarity of the story's symbolic shape.

II

Like many artists, London not only unconsciously exploited his own best talent but also consciously overexploited it on the one hand and neglected it on the other. Overexploitation occurs in a number of stories in which London consciously used the fable/parable form. In these works, of which "The Apostate" and "The Strength of the Strong" are perhaps the best known examples, London the ideologue is too fully in control of the mechanism of the story; that is, London as parablist dominates London as fabulist. "The Apostate," for example, was subtitled *A Child Labor Parable* in its magazine appearance,[5] and that is what it is—no more and no less. The story tells us, in its account of a young man who has worked from childhood in various mills and factories, that the effort to turn children and men into machines will breed rebellion, that the human body and soul are incapable of being fully mechanized. The parable is effective in its own right, but its success is on a lower level than that of "The Chinago." In that story the moralism inherent in the fable/parable form is rendered wryly rather than "preachingly." In "The Chinago," an innocent is also destroyed by "the system"—the bureaucracy of a judicial process which grinds to its conclusion even though the wrong man is being guillotined. The "way of the world" fabulist irony of the story—that for most men it is more important to get the job done and to do it well (the executioners take pride in the guillotine they have constructed) than to achieve justice—saves the story from the sermonizing effect of "The Apostate." This is not to say that "The Chinago" and "To Build a Fire" are not moral works; if their moralism were not preeminent, they would not be fables/parables. Rather it is to say that their moralism is less instructive (correct this evil) than informative (this is the way the world is) and that their tone is less indignant and somber than wry and detached.

London prefaced "The Strength of the Strong" with a brief epigraph: "Parables don't lie, but liars will parable." He attributed this aphorism to "Lip-King," and thus paid mock homage to the principal writer of fables and parables of his day, Kipling. (Indeed, Kipling is also present in the story itself in the figure of the "Bug," a poet and parablist who endorses the imperialist, capitalistic ethic of the tribal leaders.) Like "The Apostate," "The Strength of the Strong" has its origin in London's socialist convictions. The narrator of the story is one of the few survivors of a prehistoric tribe which was destroyed by its own selfish bickering. His account of tribal history is thus a history of civilization in which the parable moral is that when group interest is sacrificed to self-interest, the group is doomed. Whereas "The Apostate" lacks vitality, "The Strength of the Strong" is enlivened by the satiric edge of London's translation of various moments in Western history into comically rendered incidents in the history of a specific tribe. Nevertheless, the central thrust of the story is still that of a political sermon, of London offering a conscious rebuttal to the "Bug's" view of man's social nature and destiny. It is London's proselytizing for a cause which also vitiates his major exercise in the fully conscious parable, *The Iron Heel*. Although the novel is often described as an anti-Utopia, it can also be profitably considered a parable despite its length. As in all of London's intentional parables, the "lesson" of *The Iron Heel* is single-dimensional: the forces arrayed against the achievement of social justice in America are powerful and ruthless. The work has its moments, particularly the Battle of Chicago conclusion, but its overall failure illustrates the dangers inherent in extending ideological parable beyond the brief narrative. Parable teaches best by example, but the expansiveness of *The Iron Heel* permits London too much opportunity to teach by argument in Everhard's lengthy explanations of the rightness of his cause. "The Strength of the Strong" is by far the better artistic rendering of London's social ideas because it is by far the better parable.

III

But what of one of London's most widely read novels, *The Sea-Wolf*? This compelling but seriously flawed work assumes its basic nature from London's effort to combine characteristics of the fable/parable with those of the conventional novel. The strengths of *The Sea-Wolf* (and a number of similar works in London's canon) are those of the fable/parable, the weaknesses those of the novel.

The Sea-Wolf contains a buried fable/parable which is the principal source of its fictional energy—that of the overreacher. Wolf Larsen is less a character than a type. He is the man-as-wolf who not only acts and thinks wolfishly in his single-minded gratification of self but has the mental equipment to attempt to justify his nature. But though we may agree that there are many instances of wolflike behavior and values in life, we also agree that we are not a civilization of wolves, and we are thus more gratified than surprised when a parable element of moral retribution enters the fable of a wolf among us. He who lives by the code of animal strength will die by it, as Larsen indeed does when his vigor and shrewdness are diminished by a brain tumor. We find in the Wolf Larsen portion of *The Sea-Wolf* many of the characteristics which make *The Call of the Wild* so powerful a work: distinct moral types, symbolic setting (the ship and the sea in *The Sea-Wolf*), an allegorical narrative, and the whole mix pushing toward a fable/parable combination of worldly wisdom (the strong rule) and parable moralism (but not forever).

To this fable/parable core, London added some of the conventional ingredients of the novel in the characters and experiences of Humphrey Van Weyden and Maud Brewster. Unlike Larsen, who is unchanging in his beliefs and values, they are intended to be developing characters who undergo a significant transformation through experience. Whatever their origin in the conventions of popular initiation fiction of London's day, they are taken seriously by him as "realistic" fictional characters—that is, figures whose natures and motives are probable and believable. But London's effort to shape figures of this kind fails completely, for in Hump and Maud he has in fact created standard fictional types (effete and overrefined intellectuals) who undergo standard fictional transformations (they come to an understanding and use of strength in human affairs) and who thereby receive their just reward (survival and love). In short, whereas Wolf Larsen is acceptable and powerful because he is created and functions as a fabulistic type, Hump and Maud fail because London's inadequacies as a writer of fiction lead him to formulaic constructs, including type characters. The difference between Larsen on the one hand and Hump and Maud on the other, it should be clear, does not lie in the inherent greater appeal of one kind of figure over another. Characters undergoing initiatory experiences have been one of the great staples of major world literature, while the tyrannical sea captain has been a staple of superficial romance. The difference rather lies in London's ability to depict Wolf Larsen within the conventions of the fable/parable and his inability to deal with Hump and Maud within the conventions of the novel.

IV

Much of London's best writing is autobiographical, whether in the form of autobiography with a considerable fictional element (as in *The Road* and *John Barleycorn*) or in the form of fiction which is closely autobiographical (as in *Martin Eden*). It is true that in these works the brevity of the fable/parable is sacrificed to the fullness of detail characteristic of modern autobiography. But in all other significant ways London adapts the conventions of the fable/parable to the needs of autobiographical expression and thereby achieves some striking successes. In each of his best autobiographies, London chooses a specific area of his life for representation, and in each the material of the experience is molded into a symbolic form which expresses a truth characteristic of the worldly wisdom of the fable. So in *The Road*, London's months as a hobo dramatize the process by which the concrete experience of injustice will stimulate a rebellion against it, in *John Barleycorn* his obsession with alcohol documents the limitations of human control of desire, and in *Martin Eden* his efforts to become a writer reveal that success, once gained, is not as sweet as it seemed.

Martin Eden suggests how London adapts one of the principal impulses of autobiography—to give meaning to one's life by the selective use of the material of one's life—to create a moral allegory closely related to the form of the fable/parable. In London's account of his attempt to become a successful writer, experience is good if it contributes to this goal, evil if it hinders. The work contains little complexity of characterization, even in such fully drawn figures as Ruth Morse and Russ Brissenden, and there is no plot— only obstacles, hazards, and momentary resting places in Martin's slow rise to knowledge and competency. Ruth is Martin's False Guide in this climb; he initially mistakes her for Truth because of her seeming spirituality, but he eventually realizes her weak conventionality. Brissenden is Truth—the truth that art must be rebellious—and also Martin's Fate. Brissenden's early alcoholic death and his difficulty in gaining acceptance dramatize the condition and destiny of the artist in America. Other figures are even more programmatic. Martin's sister and brother-in-law, for example, represent respectively family loyalty and grubbing materialism, while Ruth's family embodies upper class philistine smugness. Even ideas play a symbolic role in London's fable of the artist in America, since Martin's infatuation with the thought of Herbert Spencer signifies his need to find intellectual confirmation of his sense of himself as an independent being in a conforming world. Yet despite the blatancy of the allegorical mode in *Martin Eden*, the work lives because blatancy in this instance is functional within the fable/parable form of the work. Much of that which absorbs us in *Martin Eden* is attributable to its character as a fable of the American artist at odds with his world, temporarily victoriously over it, and finally defeated by it.

As in the best of his dog stories, London in *Martin Eden* (as well as in *The Road* and *John Barleycorn*) writes powerfully in the fable/parable form both because he is writing instinctively and unconsciously within the conventions of this form and because he ignores most of the conventions of the ostensible form he is writing in while drawing profitably upon others. London's strength as a writer was not so much to tell a story as to tell a story in order to demonstrate the truth of a specific moral which revealed the way of the world but which also often instructed in the way of the heart. (In *Martin Eden*, the friendship of Martin and Brissenden plays this second role.) The writer of fables and parables may not be either original or profound, but as the history of world literature demonstrates, and as London's reputation further illustrates, at his best he can engage us fully and permanently.

Notes

1. I have been aided in my understanding of the fable by Marcel Gutwirth's published Mellon lecture, *Fable* (New Orleans: Graduate School of Tulane Univ., Fall, 1980), and by B. E. Perry's "Fable," *Studium Generale*, 12 (1959): 17–37.

2. Theodore Roosevelt, "Men Who Misinterpret Nature," in *The Works of Theodore Roosevelt* (New York: Scribner, 1926), V, 368–69; reprinted from *Everybody's Magazine*, 16 (June 1907): 770–74.

3. Earle Labor, "Jack London's Mondo Cane: *The Call of the Wild* and *White Fang*," *Jack London Newsletter*, 1 (July–Dec. 1967): 213; reprinted in Labor's *Jack London* (New York: Twayne, 1974), pp. 69–81.

4. London himself claimed, after the great success of *The Call of the Wild*, that he was unaware at the time he was writing the story that he was writing an allegory. But as to the allegorical nature of the completed work, he declared, "I plead guilty." See Joan London, *Jack London and His Times* (Seattle: Univ. of Washington Pr., 1968 [1939]), p. 252.

5. *Woman's Home Companion*, 33 (Sept. 1906): 5–7, 49.

SAM S. BASKETT

Sea Change in The Sea-Wolf

Many readers of Jack London's *The Sea-Wolf* have found themselves in agreement with Ambrose Bierce's dismissal of the last half of the book. "The 'love' element," Bierce pronounced, "with its absurd suppressions and impossible proprieties, is awful. I confess to an overwhelming contempt for both the sexless lovers."[1] The undeniable achievement of the novel has been widely recognized, but it has been seen to lie principally in the characterization of Wolf Larsen as an embodiment of the Spencerian-Darwinian-Nietzschean complex of ideas at the turn of the century, with the sentimentality of "the love element" a major flaw. The recent publication of the superbly edited *The Letters of Jack London*, however, provides the impetus for reconsidering this generally accepted assessment. For the letters written during the time of the gestation and writing of the novel throw considerable light on what London was attempting.

These are the attractive early letters of the time of Jack's impulsive first marriage, his star-crossed love of Anna Strunsky, his intense yearnings toward the ideal "mate" he was determined to find in Charmian, just at the time he was writing *The Sea-Wolf.* Two phrases from the letters are particularly striking in relation to the theme of the novel: "the woman in me" (written to Anna) and "the man concealed in woman" (written to Mabel Applegarth).[2] When these and other similar statements in the letters are kept in mind, *The*

From *American Literary Realism 1870–1910* 24, no. 2 (Winter 1992): 5–22. Copyright © 1992 by McFarland & Company.

Sea-Wolf can be seen in a different perspective. Undeniably mawkish at times, "the love element" is neither contemptible nor irrelevant, actually no more sexually outrageous than the "Wolf Larsen element"; and, moreover, the lovers, *at first* expressing the attitudes of a sexually bifurcated society are eventually in rebellion against such attitudes. *The Sea-Wolf* is far ahead of its time in anticipating late twentieth-century views concerning an ideal androgynous relation between women and men.

Carolyn Heilbrun has written that androgyny "defines a condition under which the characteristics of the sexes, and the human impulses expressed by men and women, are not rigidly assigned. Androgyny seeks to liberate the individual from the confines of the appropriate."[3] This is the liberation which London seeks to embody in his developing characters; and this theme is the insistent unifying motif of the novel, to which even the vivid characterization of the Sea Wolf himself is, it becomes apparent, clearly subordinated.

London's grappling with the ideal of androgyny, although not in that terminology, is evident early on, the Mabel Applegarth letter concerning "the man concealed in woman" being dated in December 1898. This theoretical interest in the characteristics of the sexes continues in many other letters to both female and male correspondents. That his ideas are not always consistent—London is rarely to be accused of consistency—is consonant with Heilbrun's reference to the "unbounded and hence fundamentally indefinable nature of androgyny" (p. xi). At times London does seem to express the conventional sexual attitudes of his age. Even in the letter written to Anna Strunsky in February 1902, he is on the verge of mutually exclusive distinctions: " . . . the woman in me pleads, but my manhood reasons" (p. 278). The important thing to note, however, is that London is wrestling with sexist issues, as he was with racist issues throughout his career, when most of his contemporaries considered these issues resolved.

One aspect of his musings about gender relations is expressed in an April 1899 letter to Cloudsley Johns: "All my life I have sought an ideal chum. . . . I never found the man in whom the elements were so mixed that he could satisfy, or come anywhere near satisfying my ideal" (p. 63). What he values most is a "brilliant brain" and "no physical cowardice." The latter he could "forgive" in a woman, never in a man. Such statements and, to anticipate, Humphrey Van Weyden's appreciation of Wolf Larsen's masculine beauty have made London subject of conjectures concerning possible latent homosexuality. Again, Heilbrun has written tellingly: "Androgyny appears to threaten men and women even more profoundly in their sexual than in their social roles. There has been a fear . . . of homosexuality, or the appearance of homosexuality . . . as the consequence of less rigid patterns of social behavior" (pp. xi–xii).

Another letter, to Mabel in January 1899, touches on two other aspects of sexual definition: he praises Ella Wheeler Wilcox's description of the passionately good woman as one who, distinguished from "the sweetly good woman," has the capacity to sympathize with the full range of human emotions. And he cites Spinoza to the effect that "the love both of husband and wife" should be based on "chiefly liberty of mind" (p. 44).

These and many other comments are indicative of London's continuing, thoughtful interest in defining sexual identity freed from the "appropriate." This intellectual aspect should be kept in mind in reading his more intensely emotional and personally focused writing about the topic to Anna and Charmian, lest his expression be seen as merely the typically romantic idealization of a beloved by an overwrought lover. In his first letter, in December 1899, to "My Dear Miss Strunsky," although London had just met her, it seemed as if he had known her "for an age." Addressing her as a published author to a "literary aspirant," he believes that she "is given to feel the deeps and the heights of emotion in an extraordinary degree," that she "can grasp the intensity of transcendental feeling, the dramatic force of situation, as few women, or men either, can" (pp. 133–4). The following May, London having married Bessie Maddern in April, Anna's letters make "it seem as though some new energy had been projected into the world and that I cannot fail gathering part of it to myself" (p. 183). Two months later, he tells "Dear Anna," after a theoretical disagreement, that he feels "there was no inner conflict; that we were attuned, somehow; that a real unity underlaid everything. The ship, new-launched, rushes to the sea; the sliding-ways rebel in weaking creaks and groans; but sea and ship hear them not; so with us when we rushed into each other's lives—we, the real we, were undisturbed. Comrades! Ay, world without end!" (p. 198). By the end of 1900, he can write "Comrade Mind," "A white beautiful friendship?—between a man and a woman?—the world cannot imagine such a thing, would deem it as inconceivable as infinity or non-infinity" (pp. 228–9). And in April, 1901, "Large temperamentally—that is it. It is the one thing that brings us at all in touch. We have, flashed through us, you and I, each a bit of the universal, and so we draw together. And yet we are so different" (p. 244). Obviously, these are love letters, whether consciously or not on the part of the young husband, but they are the love letters of a man who is radically questioning the rigidly defined sexual roles of men and women. The collaborative debate with Anna in writing *The Kempton-Wace Letters*, beginning in August, 1900, pursues this questioning on a literary level. Ostensibly, the debate is between romantic love, in the character written by Anna, and love considered from the standpoint of scientific materialism, in the character written by Jack. But there is a firmness to Anna's letters and a romantic flair to Jack's that blur the distinctness between the positions they are taking.

The two issues came to a head, the "white beautiful friendship between a man and a woman unimaginable to the world at large" and Jack's by-now avowed love for Anna, when he received a letter in England from her, written after she had learned of Bessie's second pregnancy. Jack, completing the experience that led to *The People of the Abyss*, was crushed by Anna's understandable withdrawal. Distraught, almost incoherent, chastened, he faced the fact that he would not recognize his ideal with Anna. "And now it is all over and done with. So be it. Henceforth I shall dream romances for other people and transmute them into bread & butter" (p. 313). As a married father, he had to accept the end of the ideal relationship he had envisaged between them. As a writer, however, and as a person, he clung to the ideal he would express in fiction.

By January, 1903, he could write George Brent, his publisher,

> I am on the track of a sea story ... which shall have adventure, storm, struggle, tragedy, and love. The love-element will run throughout, as the man & woman will occupy the center of the stage pretty much all of the time.... The *motif*, however, the human motif underlying all, will be what I may call *mastery*. My idea is to take a cultured, refined, super-civilized man and woman, (whom the subtleties of artificial, civilized life have blinded to the real facts of life), and throw them into a primitive sea-environment.... The superficial reader will get the love story & the adventure; while the deeper reader will get all this, plus the bigger thing underneath.... I intend to take plenty of time over it. (pp. 337–8)

As the book progressed, and the anguish over the rupture with Anna abated, Jack, considering his marriage "eminently unsatisfactory," was on the prowl, "preparing to go to pieces" as a stage toward his separation from Bessie. He was going "to have a hell of a time, with any woman I could get hold of. I had my eyes on a dozen women," one of whom was Charmian Kittredge (p. 521). By June, however, Jack was in love with her, as intensely as he had been with Anna the summer before. Hardly an attractive picture: married for only three years, father of two little girls, and passionately declaring himself the soul mate of two other women within a period of months, unknown to his trustful wife.

Another view can be entertained, however: Jack, by his own impulsiveness, trapped in a marriage based on stereotypic sexual roles, despite his theoretical and, indeed, emotional concept of androgyny as a necessary condition for human fulfillment. Defending his action, doubtless primarily to himself, in marrying Bessie, he slides into writing *The Kempton-Wace Letters* with the highly attractive Anna Strunsky, who clearly presented not merely a fresh and more compatible love object, but the possibility for achieving his androgynous ideal. Herself attracted to Jack, Anna could write many years later after his death, "He was youth, adventure, romance. . . . He had a genius for friendship. He loved greatly and was greatly beloved."[4] As their relationship intensified, cognizant of what was involved, she withdrew. Charmian, older, experienced, attracted by the same qualities as Anna, did not withdraw. The androgynous relationship between an androgynous man and an androgynous woman he had envisioned for himself and Anna, that could never be possible with Bessie, would now be fulfilled with Charmian.

Or so they wrote each other in June/July, 1903. He loves her beautiful body and the "beautiful mind that goes with it," rejoicing in the frankness of that mind, that she had not been "coy and fluttering . . ." And then follows his highest praise: "You are more kin to me than any woman I have ever known" (pp. 369–70). In a subsequent letter, in early July, he refers to "a wonderful moment" she has given him, apparently in answer to this asseveration: Charmian had "repeated" to him, "You are more kin to me than any woman I have ever known." This expression of what she means to him Charmian had considered the "One really great thought" in the late June letter. Jack continued, this thought, "most vital to me and to my love for you, stamped our kinship irrevocably. Surely we are very One, you and I!" Then he goes on to describe his dream of the "great Man-Comrade." What he had briskly sketched to Johns four years earlier, he now expands to five paragraphs, over five hundred impassioned words, to Charmian. The writer is unmistakably pouring out his soul to the woman with whom he has just fallen in love, but, strangely, his subject is his dream of a man-comrade. In addition to typical masculine qualities, he should be fanciful, imaginative, sentimental, delicate, tender, warm—the evocation of the perfect blending of masculine and feminine qualities goes on. Earlier, London says, he had told his dream in the arms of a woman he loved and who loved him, but she grew "passionately angry." The implication is that Charmian will understand the blending of masculine and feminine qualities that are in each that is the basis of their "kinship." "Do you see, my dear one," he begins his fifth paragraph on this theme, "the man I am trying to picture for you?—an all-around man, who could weep over a strain of music, a bit of verse, and who could grapple with the fiercest life and fight good-naturedly or like a fiend as the case might be. Don't you see, dear love, the all-around man I mean?—the man who could live at the same time in the realms of fancy and of fact . . ." (pp. 370–71).

It is just at this time, of course, that London was working intensively on *The Sea-Wolf.* On July 24, he wrote George Brent that it was "about half-done" and that "it will be utterly different in theme and treatment from the stereotyped sea novel" (p. 376). On September 2, he writes soothingly to Brent that Richard Gilder, editor of *Century Magazine* in which the novel was to appear first, need not worry about a man and a woman alone on a deserted island: "the American prudes will not be shocked by the last half of the book." He gives Gilder permission to blue pencil, but the nature "of the characters themselves, will not permit of anything offensive. . . . I elected to exploit brutality with my eyes open, preferring to do it through the first half and to save the second half for something better" (p. 383).

The "something better," of course, is the ideal androgynous relationship that develops between Maud and Humphrey, in contrast to the male brutality of the first half, a brutality embodied in Wolf Larsen and highlighted by the effeminate timidity and cowardice of Mugridge and Humphrey Van Weyden himself. This theme and the treatment of it, referred to proudly by London in the July letter to Brent just cited, had been a persistent theme in London's letters to his intimate correspondents over a period of years prior to writing *The Sea-Wolf*, as the passages I have excerpted make unmistakable—the quest for an ideal androgynous relationship, if impossible in life, was to be realized in this fiction, as his despairing letter to Anna had prophesied. But then Charmian had come into the scene and, as in the writing of *The Kempton-Wace Letters*, London's quest in his fiction, in his letters, in his life became virtually indistinguishable.

* * *

With these revealing letters in mind, now to reconsider *The Sea-Wolf*. Three distinct but related aspects of Humphrey Van Weyden's characterization stand out: initially, he is deficient in "masculine" qualities; he is a philosophical idealist; and he is a highly regarded literary critic, "Dean of American Letters the Second," as Maud terms him.[5] Had London entitled the novel "The Rise of Humphrey Van Weyden," the complexity of his characterization might have received the considered attention it requires. As it is, the title and the vivid uniqueness of the Sea Wolf himself have made him loom large in the novel, overshadowing Humphrey, relatively vapid, but nonetheless the character whose transformation is central to the unifying theme adumbrated in London's letters.

At the age of thirty-five, his mother and sisters have been "always about me." His complete "innocence of the realities of life" had caused him to be nicknamed "Sissy." He has never been in love, his interest in women having always been "aesthetic and nothing more." Somewhat dissatisfied with this self image, he has "vaguely" thought of escape from "the atmosphere of women," but he has not had enough strength of will. Similarly, although he has a good physical constitution, he has never developed his body despite doctors' advice. He can't swim: his muscles are "small and soft, like a woman's." On the *Ghost*, even the offensively effeminate ship's cook calls him a "'mama's darlin'.'" Trying to recover the $185 the cook has stolen from him, "unused to violence of any sort," he cowers away from the threatened blows, shamefully recognizing that his cowardice has "smirched and sullied his manhood."

In the coarse, savage, all-male world of the *Ghost*, the crew appears to Humphrey as "a half-brute, half-human species, a race apart, wherein there is no such thing as sex; that they are hatched out by the sun like turtle-eggs, or receive life in some similar and sordid fashion. . . ." It dawns on him that he has never "placed a proper valuation upon woman kind." If these men had wives, sisters, daughters, "they would then be capable of softness, and tenderness and sympathy. As it is . . . not one of them has been in contact with a good woman, or within the influence, or redemption, which irresistibly radiates from such a creature" (pp. 128–29). This passage has been cited to show that London, despite his disavowals, holds to the stereotypical views of the role of "good" women as redeemers of the male, further proof that the novel, the "Larsen element" apart, is a conventional sentimental romance. It should be remembered, however, that it is the sexually discredited Humphrey—not the Jack London whose letter distinguishes between the "sweetly" and "passionately" good woman—who utters these thoughts, and that he is confusedly ambivalent about his own feminization—he has tried to "escape" from his mother and sisters. In other words, the "over-civilized" Humphrey can only envisage redeeming falseness by falseness—brute masculinity by sentimentalized femininity. That he doesn't really believe in such a redemption is strikingly evident in his perhaps unconscious contempt for the halfworld of sentimental femininity expressed as the ferry is sinking. A "preternatural[ly] calm" passenger, an ex-sailor with artificial legs, comments, "'listen to the women scream,' he said grimly—almost bitterly, I thought, as though he had been through the experience before." Contrastingly, the women are "hysterical" as the "calm" man fastens life jackets about them. The fear of death upon them, they made sounds that remind Humphrey, by now "becoming hysterical myself," "of the squealing of pigs under the knife of the butcher, and I was struck with horror at the vividness of the analogy" (pp. 6–7). Neither a strictly feminine approach, historically susceptible to reductive sentimentalization in a male-controlled society, nor a strictly masculine approach, historically susceptible to brutalization in that society, is adequate as even Humphrey intermittently recognizes. But his insufficient realization of either genuine femininity or genuine masculinity is a mark of his Prufrockian incapacity in both thought and action.

Before he can understand true femininity and make it a part of his total androgynous sexual being, Humphrey must first "escape" his effeminacy; and a step in the right direction is his realization that Larsen will not help him recover the stolen money: "Whatever was to be done I must do for myself" (p. 90). He does overcome the effeminate Mugridge, but only "out of the courage of fear." In this *pas de deux* of two weaklings, Humphrey learns to see himself more accurately.

His next tutor is Wolf Larsen. Hump, as Larsen renames him, is attracted to the extent that many have seen suggestions of latent homosexuality in the character—and in his creator. As Heilbrun observed, to a man with an impulse toward androgyny, the label of homosexuality is always a threat. In context, however, the label can be seen as invalid. Hump does recognize Wolf's "elemental" strength, "a thing apart from his physical semblance." But this strength is the "potency of motion" which "lingers in a shapeless lump of turtle-meat and recoils and quivers from the prod of a finger" (pp. 18–19). The echo of the turtle imagery should be remarked—the description of the crew in the womanless world of the *Ghost*—a world in which "there is no such thing as sex." In effect, London gives the newly rechristened Hump the dawning realization that masculinity with no admixture of feminine qualities is asexual. Similarly, the same point is repeatedly made regarding sentimentalized femininity in the face of physical danger or the raw realities of life. If such men are like turtles hatched by the sun, such women are like squealing pigs under the knife. Hump's own "hysteria" and his effeminacy suggest that he, too, initially, has no sex.

On the *Ghost*, Hump slowly claims an androgynous sexuality partly through his appreciation of Larsen. Acting effectively in the stereotypically feminine role of "nurse," dressing Larsen's wounds after the forecastle fight, Hump describes him as the "man-type, the masculine, and almost a god in his perfectness." This seemingly "aesthetic" appreciation is undercut by the immediately following description of "the great muscles [that] leapt and moved under the satiny skin. . . . His body, thanks to his Scandinavian stock, was as fair as the fairest woman's. . . . I could not take my eyes off him," "watching his biceps move like a living thing under its white sheath." Much has been made of this passage, but to reduce it simplistically to homoeroticism is to ignore London's careful treatment. Shortly before this scene, a crew member has stated that Hump is "'all right. . . . He don't like the old man no more than you or me.'" Immediately prior to the description just quoted, Hump makes a contrasting reference to the "powerfully muscled" but physically flawed crew. There is "only one whose lines were at all pleasing, while in so far as they pleased, that far had they been what I should call feminine." Then begins the description of Larsen's "masculine" physique. But in the midst of this description a different note is sounded. These are the biceps "that had nearly crushed out my life once, that I had seen strike so many killing blows." And immediately after the passage, when Hump tries to relate Larsen's well-made body to "purpose," Larsen dismisses the idea: "'Purpose? Utility is the better word.'" Hump's conclusion makes clear that whatever the physical masculine perfection, Larsen's stark manhood is insufficient to him. At this point he backs away from arguing teleologically, but he does dehumanize the Sea Wolf's masculinity in an effective metaphor: "I had seen the mechanism of the primitive fighting beast, and I was as strongly impressed as if I had seen the engines of a great battleship . . ." (pp. 141–4). To achieve full manhood, Hump, reductively feminized by his society, must grow beyond Thomas Mugridge; he cannot accept the crew in their brutishness signified by their actions and physical malformations; and even the physically magnificent Wolf Larsen is ultimately an inadequate model. Developing a better understanding of manhood, he can see raw, unmitigated masculinity for what it is. He is surely appreciative of Larsen's "godlike" physique, his strength of mind, but he is even more repelled by his brutish actions and his militant philosophical materialism.

Larsen's explanation of the "purpose" of his beautifully muscled body is "stability, equilibrium"—he has "legs to stand on," in specific contrast to Humphrey. "'You stand on dead men's legs,'" he had taunted on learning of an inherited income. Hump does come to stand on his own legs, learning to function effectively as the "mate" of the *Ghost*. But he must also learn to stand on his own legs philosophically, and this he does in pitting his idealism against the other's radical materialism. Larsen envisages life as like yeast, "a ferment, a thing that moves . . . but that in the end will cease to move . . . something which devour[s] life that it might live"; and living is "merely successful piggishness" (pp. 50–2). Hump finds Larsen's materialism "compelling." "Not that I," he protests to himself, "a confirmed . . . idealist,—was to be compelled: but that Wolf Larsen stormed the last strongholds of my faith with a vigor that received respect, while not accorded conviction" (p. 83).

Reiterated rebirth imagery emphasizes that Hump's change is nothing less than a complete transformation, physically, psychologically and philosophically from the hollow man he had essentially been beneath a facade of superficial achievement and conventional understanding. His rebirth could scarcely be stated more explicitly: The story begins on a January morning, Monday, a new year, a new day. The "Dean of American Letters the Second" is "pulled" from the water (he had been unable to "cry out") and, gradually regaining consciousness, becomes aware of a "mighty rhythm . . . the lift and plunge of the ship." He catches his breath "painfully," opens his eyes, sees his body bloody from chafing hands attempting to force air into his lungs. He is on the *Ghost*—the name emphasizes that it is indeed another world into which he has been pulled. Humphrey Van Weyden, literary critic, is given a new name; he learns "to walk" on the ship; he receives repeated "impresses from the die which had stamped the crew"; he loses his "innocence," seeming to find in Wolf Larsen's forbidding philosophy "a more adequate explanation of life than I found in my own." He finds it remarkable that the literary specialist he has been can function as a sailor. But his change is yet more fundamental. He begins to feel

> that I could never be quite the same man I had been. While my hope and faith in human life still survived Wolf Larsen's destructive criticism . . . he had opened up for me the world of the real, of which I had known practically nothing and from which I had always shrunk. I had learned to look more closely at life as it was lived, to recognize that there were such things as facts in the world, to emerge from the realm of the mind and idea and to place certain values on the concrete and objective phases of existence (p. 156).

Recently, Joseph Boone has interestingly compared *The Sea-Wolf* with *Moby Dick*, *Huckleberry Finn* and *Billy Budd*.[6] Boone notes that the texts of Melville and Twain explore the realization within men themselves of emotions and values traditionally associated with women, that the union of androgynous attributes takes place internally, but that in *The Sea-Wolf* it is external, with Maud Brewster representing the feminine component of the androgynous union. But it seems clear that Hump has, to a considerable extent, achieved such a union before Maud appears, having shed his superficial, and essentially false, effeminacy and having become more "manly" in the transformation detailed through the course of the novel.

And so, as one might expect from London's letters expressing his desire for an ideal female comrade as well as male as essential for a full life, Maud Brewster appears in the middle of the Darwinian sea. Charles Watson in his valuable analysis of *The Sea-Wolf* has observed that the central action "involves a crisis of sexual as well as intellectual identity. In this crisis, 'masculinity' implies both homosexuality and nihilism (the creed of brute strength), while 'femininity' implies heterosexuality and ethical idealism . . . Humphrey must pass through an intermediate stage of masculine exclusivity before arriving at a final stage of sexual and psychological adulthood."[7] This is an admirably succinct abstraction of some of the major issues—and the cultural, sexual and psychological undertones of those issues. But such reductions take too little notice of the careful and convincing way in which London has sketched Hump's development as a person, not as an abstract idea, a personal element which London's letters about ideal male and female roles alert the reader not to slight. In reading the novel, Hump must be seen as a person, whatever the author's shortcomings in making him believable; on the other hand, whatever the author's success in embodying in the Sea Wolf powerful contemporary ideas, he is never faintly credible as a person. Moreover, it seems to me that, similarly, Watson takes too little account of Maud Brewster's role in this connection. He does state that Maud, although unconvincing, enables London to preserve "a certain theoretical consistency in choosing a sexual and philosophical equilibrium for the woman as well as the man" (p. 76). But she is more significant in the resolution of the novel than this passing "theoretical" nod suggests. Admittedly, at times she is at once unconvincing and painfully conventional, indicative of London's problem in presenting her and what he does to resolve it. London had to create not the female persona implicit in his letters to Anna and Charmian, but one that Editor Gilder and the "American prudes" would accept. As she is delineated, Maud is central in Hump's crisis of identity which involves a social identity.

The three opening paragraphs of the chapter immediately preceding the one in which Maud appears give the only detailed description of the mission of the *Ghost*—killing seals for their pelts. By now, Hump is "mate," "handling and directing" the crew in their bloody tasks on the decks "covered with hides and bodies," although his soul and stomach are "revolted." And yet "Sissy" Van Weyden considers his position "wholesome" as he improves his "executive" abilities. In the same passage he comments that this "wanton slaughter" was in order that the skins "might later adorn the fair shoulders of the women of the cities" (p. 155).

On first reading, these paragraphs seem unlike anything else in the book, and yet in them London skillfully brings three strands of the novel together. Hump, now capable of dealing with "the world of the real," contrasts sharply with the effete litterateur of the opening chapter relishing his role as a specialist, smugly comfortable in his not having to know anything of the objective world about him. Moreover, he is now able to offer social criticism. In the opening scene he complacently accepted "the division of labor," the status quo in which he could publish in the *Atlantic*, the officers could sail the ferry across San Francisco Bay and a passenger could read the article. But now he sees the division of labor differently. Hump, before the *Ghost*, could not have perceived as much. This social criticism relates to another apparently incongruous passage, in which Wolf Larsen uncharacteristically explains himself in social terms. Unlike Hump, with an inherited income, he had only his own legs to stand on. Hump has strengthened his physical legs, but he also is now able to understand Larsen's social criticism—and this is central to the novel—in sexual terms: brutish men kill revoltingly to survive in a social scheme in which hypocritically "civilized" men buy the results of their "wanton slaughter" to bedeck the "fair shoulder" of their women in an economically inequitable and sexually bifurcated society in which women are kept in parasitic dependence.

In the next chapter Maud enters the novel, however unbelievably. Hump's conventional idealization of her as he falls in love is often embarrassingly evident in both his vocabulary and attitudes, seeming to support Boone's assertion that a "model shift from quest format to erotic-seduction narrative accompanying Maud's arrival serves to underscore London's vision of 'correct' male behavior" (p. 206). Care must be taken, however, to distinguish the character, even as he has been transformed in his masculinity, from the author. The point has been insistently made that all his life Hump has been "surrounded" by women in a feminized culture, but also apart from them—viewing them stereotypically. There has been no basis for a complete transformation of his understanding in the all-male world of the *Ghost*, although the social-sexual criticism cited above provides hints of his awakening. That London is attempting to create a character undergoing change rather than representing his own views of women is suggested by the contrast between Hump's mawkish effusions and even London's most passionate letters to Anna and Charmian. Moreover, under this mawkishness, due to whatever complex of failures—personal, artistic, and cultural—different notes are sounded as London develops the relation between the characters in terms of their mutual androgyny.

As the *Ghost* approaches the small boat carrying Maud, it is thought to be the craft in which two crew members had tried to flee Larsen's persecution, and Hump, surely for the first time in his life takes a loaded shotgun in his hands, intending to confront Larsen. Yet this scene also skillfully indicates how far Hump has still to grow. As the *Ghost* comes closer, one of the crew gives a curious exclamation. "'May I never shoot a seal again if that ain't a woman!'" (p. 176)—a remark which, along with Hump's action, ties the male seal-shooting world and women together in their distinct separation, as in the passage cited from the previous chapter; but even as they are yoked in this exotic scene, the sexual bifurcation is emphasized—a version of the sexual attitudes characteristic of the society, the society which had shaped Humphrey Van Weyden, literary critic. After four months at sea, "We," Hump thus includes himself with the crew, "were agog with excitement" at a woman in their male midst. But to the crew she is simply a sexual object, as is to be enacted in Larsen's subsequent attempted rape, while to Hump, she is "like a being from another world," the world he had previously known—and yet not really known. He forgets his "mate's duties," so enraptured is he by her conventionally ethereal femininity: "It seemed to me that I was realizing for the first time what a delicate, fragile creature a woman is . . ." (p. 178). This is to cite only one of a host of his conventional rhapsodic effusions.

Thus neither the crew nor Hump sees Maud accurately. The crew sees her ultimately in terms of lust. And Hump's transformation has not included his conventionally sentimental attitude toward women. But somewhat later in looking back on his first reaction to Maud's presence, he reflects, "All this, in frankness, to show my first impression, after long denial, of women in general and of Maud Brewster in particular" (p. 178). The sentence is far from clear, but it may be read that from some time later Hump is self-critically looking back to his first impression of Maud, "in frankness." He offers as reason for his inaccurate first impression "the long denial" of women, which could refer to the womanless life on the *Ghost*—or his long conventional, "aesthetic" consideration of women, in effect a life-long "denial" of women as they really are. Further, since there has been no long denial of Maud, his first impression of her is the same as his first, conventional impression of women in general, which he now must admit—"in frankness"—is wrong. As he had been wrong in his feelings about what constituted manhood, so he had been wrong about womanhood.

In part, the development toward androgyny after Maud enters the novel is in terms of Hump's better understanding of her; in part, it is in changes in Maud herself. Their backgrounds are the same. She is a highly civilized, well-regarded writer in the sexually bifurcated society that the two have shared. She has published several "thin" volumes of poetry which Humphrey had read appreciatively, including a "perfect sonnet," "A Kiss Endured." Like him, she is an unreflecting idealist. However, she is more than merely conventional, expressing considerable confidence and courage in stark circumstances, even though she is "unaccustomed to the vagrant, careless life" of the *Ghost*. At first, naively, she is "perturbed . . . but not frightened" when she learns that her "simple faith" that "shipwrecked people are always shown every consideration" is a "misconception" (p. 178). When she learns of Larsen's "man-play" during which a shark bites off the cook's leg, she does not faint as Hump expects, but "controls herself." She can understand that this may have been "largely an accident." But she cannot condone Hump's failure to try to prevent the murder of the two crew members through "moral courage [which] is never without effect," even as she totally rejects the idea of killing Larsen. Hump responds that moral courage is "worthless . . . on this little floating world," as is all her previous experience. As he advises her to dissemble, Larsen approaches and Hump turns the conversation to the literary world and the lack of "moral courage" of editors "afraid" of publishing a certain writer—perhaps London's concealed swipe at Editor Gilder, albeit on another, if similar, floating world.

In any event, despite her previous "faith," her unwillingness to lie "by speech and action," she follows his advice and does dissemble.

As Larsen's sexual intentions become increasingly obvious, Maud is "terrified," but not "hysterical," and Hump admiringly notes that there is a considerable amount of "robust clay in her constitution." When the *Ghost* is attacked by Death Larsen, she calmly states that she intends to show Wolf that "we are as brave as he," bringing forth his appreciative and pointedly sexual comment: "'Books, and brains, and bravery. You are well rounded . . . fit to be the wife of a pirate chief'" (p. 233). Hump, having realized his love for her and the danger she is in with Larsen, remarks, observing them together, "Each was nothing that the other was, everything that the other was not . . . and I likened them to the extreme ends of the human ladder of evolution— the one the culmination of all savagery, the other the finished product of the finest civilization" (p. 213). It is easy to read in this and similar outpourings the elements of the conventional sentimental romance that many have seen the novel becoming. The fair maiden is threatened with violation by the villain; unalloyed femininity by brutal masculinity; idealism by unprincipled materialism—with Hump as hero to save all. But the complex implications of these oppositions go beyond the melodramatic dimensions. Even London's bald but skillful metaphor—"A Kiss Endured" versus rape—suggests the ambivalences. Maud is not yet, the novel makes clear, "a finished product" discerned by Hump when she comes aboard the *Ghost*. The "finest civilization," where both Maud and Hump have earned their laurels, where "a kiss" is sentimentalized, is a pallid world as Hump is coming to realize: given his transformation, on his return he will be unable to live in that world on the same basis as before, as London's letters as well as the novel surely suggest. And given his transformation, his ability to function in Larsen's world, he will be unable to deny what he has achieved on the *Ghost*. Also Maud out of her complete experience is hardly likely to write another "Kiss Endured," but will write of love given in honesty rather than sentimentality, as the closing sentence of the book makes explicit in Maud's frank expression of sexual desire. These are the strands of masculinity and femininity which London seeks to bring together in androgynous resolution to the love story and to the novel.

In terms of the action of the novel, Hump is able to rescue Maud, as they escape to the open seas and eventually to Endeavor Island, where indeed they will "try" together to make, as man and woman, the best of the new world in which they find themselves. From the time they leave the *Ghost*, they are increasingly "similarly affected," each more and more closely attuned to the "subjective" consciousness of the other, in contrast to Larsen's focus on "the immediate, objective present." As they launch into the open sea, in effect they plight their troth in an exchange reminiscent of that between Jack and Charmian quoted previously: Maud says, "'you are a brave man'"; Hump answers, "'it is you who are a brave woman'" (p. 257). Instead of separating their roles, this exchange unites them in their bravery facing life and death on the open ocean, their fates sexually indistinguishable. Maud learns to steer the small boat and protects Hump by allowing him to sleep, even as he has sought to protect her; and Hump sees her as "woman, my kind, on my plane, and the delightful intimacy of kind, of man and woman, was possible, as well as the reverence and awe in which I knew I should always hold her" (p. 261), a description of androgynous gender relations which anticipates the conclusion of Sherwood Anderson's "Sophistication" a decade or so later: "Man or boy, woman or girl, they had for a moment taken hold of the thing that makes the mature life of man and woman, in the modern world possible"—that indeed Hemingway was trying "to take hold of" fictionally in *A Farewell to Arms* and *The Garden of Eden* in the decades ahead. When Maud says that they will "'stand watches just as they do on ships,'" Hump replies, "'I don't see how I am to teach you.... I am just learning for myself.'" Maud answers, "'Then we'll learn together ...'" (p. 262). As Hump's undeclared love is increasing, they also become "good comrades, and we grew better comrades as the days went by." Although even a "robust woman" would have been frightened by "the terrible sea, the frail boat, the storms, the suffering, the strangeness and isolation of the situation," all this "seemed to make no impression upon her who had known life only in its most sheltered and consummately artificial aspects ..." (p. 271). Fully aware of their predicament, she remained "sure of permanence in the changing order of the universe." The contrast with the earlier "squealing" women is striking.

Ashore, Maud helps Hump to build the *two* huts, the separation necessitated, it should be remembered, by Editor Gilder's fears regarding the book-buying public, but it does emphasize their complementary androgyny as Hump, "alone in my little hut," thinks that "a tie, or a tacit something, existed between us which had not existed before" (p. 297). Maud even gives advice, learned from reading David Starr Jordan and from conversation with Larsen, on how to deal with the seals, and leads the assault for the skins with which to make a roof: from this knowledge, they seek out the "young bulls, living out the loneliness of their bachelorhood and gathering strength against the day when they would fight their way into the ranks of the benedicts," much as Hump himself has been doing (p. 291). Hump's adoring celebration, "my woman, my mate [which] kept ringing in my head," indeed smacks of the saccharine, but less so in the context of his full awareness of her role in their survival and his recognition that she was "living the life of a savage and living it quite successfully." As such a woman, she has contributed to his "manhood, rooting it deeper and sending through it the sap of a new strength" (p. 308).

Thus her non-feminine contributions to their endeavors on the island are verbally reinforced by sexual innuendo and this passage would seemingly be as far as London could go in this direction under Gilder's editorial eye.

But not so. Maud's greatest physical assistance is in stepping the mast on the wrecked *Ghost*. She is absolutely essential in the operation as it is described in terms which London must have enjoyed getting by Gilder. Maud recognizes that the mast suspended in the air by the "shears-tackle" which had originally failed because of its "shortness," is "'not over the hole. . . . Will you have to begin all over?'" But with Hump's "instructions for lowering away," the "butt of the mast" after several carefully defined adjustments is perfectly fitted. In the

> lantern light, we peered at what we had accomplished. We looked at each other, and our hands felt their way and clasped. The eyes of both of us . . . were moist with the joy of success.
>
> "It was done so easily after all," I remarked. "All the work was in the preparation.
>
> "And all the wonder in the completion," Maud added. "I can scarcely bring myself to realize that that great mast is really up and in; that you have lifted it . . . swung it through the air, and deposited it here where it belongs." (pp. 348–50)

Whether or not the author of "A Kiss Endured" was conscious of what she was saying, unquestionably the Charmian of the letters must have relished what her lover had written. It remains for the two thus accomplished lovers in their androgynous completion, to which the entire novel has been pointing, to deal with Larsen and return from Endeavour Island to society. Larsen in his blindness yet attempts to kill Hump and burn the ship, but he soon dies, an undaunted materialist, his final word, "'Bosh!'" As they bury him at sea, symbolically disposing of the extremity of his brutish masculinity, Maud, still the idealist but from the breadth of understanding she has achieved, whispers, "'Good-by, Lucifer, proud spirit . . . '"[8]—no longer the sweetly good woman but the passionately good woman in Wilcox's distinction admired by London in the January 1899 letter.

In Boone's analysis of *The Sea-Wolf* in relation to other quest romances mentioned previously, he sees the imminent return of Hump and Maud to civilization as "transforming the text's originally infinity-bound quest into a circular return and a recuperation of the familiar." In contrast to other quest romances, Boone asserts, this return thus thematically supports "an already existing ethos" of conventional gender roles and textually is evidence of London's failure "in maintaining the open-ended imperatives of the [quest] mode" as he concludes the novel with the happy ending of the sentimental romance (p. 209). In comparing *The Sea-Wolf* to these other works, Boone underscores dimensions for which London has not always been given credit, although Watson has observed that at a time when *Moby Dick* was nearly forgotten, *The Sea-Wolf* is evidence that London "read it more creatively than any novelist had yet done, building on its major motifs and absorbing the literary tradition that lies behind it" (p. 61). But Boone's conclusion that the novel falls short in these comparisons needs further examination. One does not have to claim that London's achievement is on a level with that of Melville and Twain—or even overlook what Watson calls the "saccharine conventionality" which too often characterizes the narrator's language and attitude in telling the love story—to see that *The Sea-Wolf* maintains both a thematic and a textual integrity. Clearly Hump and Maud during their sea voyage have experienced a change toward androgyny. They are both quite different in themselves as well as in relation to each other. And surely Boone overstates when he says that in contrast to the "independent identities" of Ishmael or Huck or Billy, Hump and Maud are dependent on each other. As London's letters reiterate, and as the development of the characters supports, he is interested in showing a man and a woman who complement each other in an ideal androgynous union because each has a sense of individual identity that transcends conventional concepts of gender roles. Moreover, the writer of the letters, one who for many years signed himself "Yours for the Revolution," was desirous of a transformed society based on individuals freed from fallacious and debilitating conventionality.

Such a motif is explicitly evident throughout the novel. At the end Hump and Maud are fitted to live with each other, both personally and professionally (as literary critic and poet), no longer controlled, even intellectually and emotionally encapsulated, as each had been earlier, in what Ann Douglas has termed a feminized American culture. In effect, then, the quest motif, with its metaphysical implications, is united with the theme of androgyny, with its social implications. The quest is not so much abandoned as given a potential social dimension, a dimension that has never been sufficiently recognized—in part, it must be admitted, because London offers only scattered hints concerning the involvement of Hump and Maud on their return to society that had warped not only them but Wolf Larsen as well. The hints are there, however, as in *The Sea-Wolf* London in a textual innovation merges the quest romance with the social novel as Fitzgerald was to do a generation later in *The Great Gatsby*. London had promised Brent something "utterly different" in his novel. Whatever its flaws, London delivered on his promise, achieving a significant highly original thematic and textual contribution to the American literary canon.

Notes

1. *The Letters of Ambrose Bierce*, ed. Bertha Clark Pope (San Francisco: Book Club of California, 1922), p. 105.

2. *The Letters of Jack London, Volume 1: 1896–1905*, eds. Earle Labor, Robert C. Leitz, III and I. Milo Shepard (Stanford, CA: Stanford Univ. Press, 1988) 36, 278. Subsequent page references in text.

3. Carolyn Heilbrun, *Toward a Recognition of Androgyny* (New York: Alfred A. Knopf, 1973) p. x. Subsequent page references in text.

4. "Memories of Jack London," *The Bowery News* (June 1962), 8–9.

5. *The Sea-Wolf* (New York: The Macmillan Company, 1904), p. 199. Subsequent page references in text.

6. "Male Independence and the American Quest Genre: Hidden Sexual Politics in the All-Male Worlds of Melville, Twain and London," in *Gender Studies: New Directions in Feminist Criticism*, ed. Judith Spector (Bowling Green, OH: Bowling Green State Univ. Popular Press, 1986). Subsequent page references in text.

7. Charles N. Watson, *The Novels of Jack London: A Reappraisal* (Madison: Univ. of Wisconsin Press, 1983), p. 65. Subsequent page references in text.

8. In thus recognizing Larsen's dimensions, Maud moves, in Heilbrun's terms, beyond what she might have earlier considered "appropriate," a development that is also suggested in the last sentence of the novel: Maud's smile, as she "completed" Hump's expression of love, is "whimsical with love," "whimsical as I had never seen it," recalling an earlier description of Larsen's "whimsical" smiles, the only other appearance of this word in the text (p. 142).

JONATHAN AUERBACH

"Congested Mails": Buck and Jack's "Call"

Frustrated by a recalcitrant Congress, President Theodore Roosevelt in 1907 sought to divert himself by playing the role of literary critic. He took as his texts—no surprise—animal tales, among them the dog stories of Jack London. Lumping London together with popular boys' writers such as W. J. Long, Roosevelt dismissed these authors as mystifying "nature-fakers." If London and these others really understood nature, Roosevelt charged, they wouldn't go about humanizing animals in such preposterous and unbeliev-able ways. Taking on Roosevelt in an essay published the next year, London countered by accusing the President of being "homocentric," a rank "ama-teur" unschooled in the principles of evolution that insist on an intimate "kinship" or strict unbroken continuity between animals and humans. Early in the article London does admit a crucial difference—that his "dog-heroes" were "not directed by abstract reasoning." But he points out that he "clogged his narrative" and violated his "artistic canons" with such phrases as "He did not think these things; he merely did them" in order to emphasize this difference, rather than cover it up, as Roosevelt implied.[1]

Teddy and Jack challenging each other's authority about (and over) nature. My aim here is not to settle this rivalry between one of America's most flamboyant and virile presidents and one of its most flamboyant and virile writers, a dispute that is being waged today in more sophisticated ways

From *American Literature* 67, no. 1 (March 1995): 51–76. Copyright © 1995 by Duke University Press.

among sociobiologists, cultural constructivists, animal rights activists, and others.[2] Although it is difficult to imagine what sort of representation of nature could avoid being "homocentric," it seems equally naive to attempt to measure London's "dog-heroes" against some absolute standard of verisimilitude, as Roosevelt would. A more central issue is the peculiar narrative self-consciousness alluded to by London that attends the directing of his animal-protagonists. Reviving the dispute the following year (1909), the critic Frederic Taber Cooper makes the point nicely:

> There is a vast difference between thinking of man as a healthy human animal and thinking of him as an unhealthy human beast— and the Call-of-the-Wild school of fiction is tending toward precisely this exaggerated and mistaken point of view. The chief trouble with all the so-called Back-to-Nature books is that they suggest an abnormal self-consciousness, a constant preoccupation regarding the measure of our animalism. Now, it is a sort of axiom that so long as we are healthy and normal, we do not give much thought to our physical machinery. . . . But this, in a certain way, is precisely what the characters in the average Call-of-the-Wild novel seem to be doing, or at least what the authors are constantly doing for them. They seem, so to speak, to keep their fingers insistently upon the pulse of their baser animal emotions—and this is precisely what the primitive, healthy savage is furtherest removed from doing.[3]

Deftly conventionalizing London's narratives as already part of a literary "school" by means of those three hyphens, Cooper raises the key issue of self-consciousness but mistakes a cause for an effect. Introspection in London is not simply some abnormal, degenerate end-stage alternative to "healthy savage" human animalism but rather a logical prerequisite for such natural primitivism, manifesting itself most starkly (as Cooper's wording suggests) in the confusion between what his characters seem to be doing and what London as narrator does *for* them. In this sense the entire concept of nature that underwrites the literary naturalism of London is fundamentally "faked," to borrow Roosevelt's memorable phrase.

Tracing the reversion of a domesticated dog to a savage wolf-beast in the primitive Yukon, London manages in fact to address a set of "unnatural" cultural issues in *The Call of The Wild* (1903): vocational training, the quest for social approval via diligent work, the material conditions of literary production, and the meaning of fame. These complex concerns all center on the practice of writing, I will argue, following the lead of a number of recent studies that seek in various ways to revise the prevailing understanding of American literary naturalism as a mode grounded in deterministic laws of environment and biology. Christopher Wilson, for example, makes a compelling case for Progressive Era writers, including London, as participating in an emerging culture of professionalism that treated writing as a discipline and business. Wilson's excellent study does not, however, discuss in any detail how such vocational concerns are enacted in the fiction itself—my emphasis throughout this essay.[4]

Written at a crucial juncture in London's career, just as his apprenticeship work in magazines was beginning to attract a wider national audience, *The Call of the Wild* dramatizes London's own struggle to gain recognition as a writer. Reading the dog Buck's "calling" as a mail carrier in the light of his author's aspirations, I further hope to show how London's narrative is important insofar as it renders literal what a trio of influential critics (Walter Benn Michaels, Michael Fried, and Mark Seltzer) have recently identified as a particular thematics of naturalist writing—texts which tend to draw attention to their own peculiar status as material marks. But while these critics treat such writing strictly in terms of its production, I will be suggesting finally that London is more interested in how writing gets published, how the artist/dog makes a name for himself once letters are circulated and delivered in the wild.[5]

To analyze London's constructing of nature in *The Call of the Wild* we need to begin by examining more closely Buck's double status as "dog-hero," as well as the related vexed doubling of character and narrator. Most critics rely on terms such as "anthropomorphism," "beast fable," and/or "allegory" to explain Buck, but the technical representation of an animal center of consciousness and the rhetorical *effects* of such a center are more complicated (and interesting) than these terms generally allow. Look at London's verbs, for instance. It is easy enough to compile a list of mental actions attributed to Buck that would seem problematic, to say the least: at various points in the narrative, Buck is said to "imagine" (7), "decide" (9), "realize" (9), "know" (9), "divine" (10), "wonder" (12), and so on, over and above London's catchall convenient phrases "dimly aware" (7) and "feel vaguely" (50).[6] These relatively innocent epistemological quirks centering on matters of cognition are presumably inevitable, to invoke London's own accusation about Roosevelt's "homocentrism." But very early on in the narrative these verbs are crucial for giving the reader a basis for identifying with Buck as a thinking presence who is on occasion disturbed by dreams and memories, as when the "scene" of Curly's death returns to trouble his sleep (16), or when he stares into a fire and "[thinks] of Judge Miller's big house" (41) and then reviews other scenes of his recent past.

To be fair, London usually takes scrupulous pains to avoid such unmediated access to Buck, achieving in the process a far more ambiguous and complex representation of his dog-hero. When Buck is initially caged, for instance, London writes, "he could not understand what it all meant" (8), followed by two interrogatives. As in the case of Norris's *McTeague*, it is uncertain whether these free-floating questions belong to character or to narrator thinking for him; the result is a mental state that belongs exclusively neither to Buck nor Jack, but seems shared somewhere between them. London's use of the modal "could" in the sentence above reinforces this ambiguity: is Buck's lack of understanding a structural incapacity stemming from his nature as dog or only a temporary limitation to be overcome by greater force of insight or knowledge when the "meaning" of his experience would become available to him? As we shall shortly see, this sort of question is crucial once we move from the static representation of Buck to consider how he is directed as "hero," how he and his mind grow and change as London plots for him.

Before looking at *The Call*'s plotting, it will be useful to consider briefly some precursor texts, the better to zero in on the peculiarities of London's animal tale. Two extremely popular immediate precursors are most pertinent here: Kipling's *Jungle Book* (1893) and Ernest Thompson Seton's *Wild Animals I Have Known* (1898).[7] Drawing on a literary tradition that extends back to Chaucer and beyond, Kipling's Mowgli stories are beast fables, filled with "Mother Wolves and Father Wolves" commenting wisely about quite complex social rules and regulations—"The Law of the Jungle." Clearly the effect of having animals speak in their own (human) voices is quite different from London's narrating for his mute hero. Like most beast fables, Kipling's talking animals serve to defamiliarize the human world (babies are "naked cubs"); when London on occasion tries such an effect, for example referring to gold in his opening paragraph as "yellow metal" (5), the results are feeble, for he's clearly not really interested in using his dog to make humans seem strange; if anything, it is the natural realm, not the cultural, which gets progressively defamiliarized during the narration.

Thompson Seton writes beast fables for children as well, often substituting a native American Indian mythos for Kipling's Orientalism. Seton also writes about animals in a naturalist vein closer to London than London perhaps cared to admit in his 1908 response to Roosevelt's accusations. Like Buck and his sledmates, Seton's "wild animals I have known" are heavily invested with character traits such as sullenness, courage, fidelity, and pride. A fierce wolf dies of a broken heart at the loss of his freedom and the loss of a beloved mate. An abandoned sheep dog spends years waiting patiently for his undeserving master, and so on. But since Thompson's narration depends simply on stringing together anecdotes, we never really see the origins or development of these humanized personalities, nor do we see how these animals interact socially with one another (a strong feature of Kipling's tales). And since he sees himself as a naturalist rather than a novelist, Seton tells his shaggy dog stories by simply attributing personality from the outside without presuming to register any internal mental states of the animals.

Neither exactly beast fable nor sentimentalized anthropomorphism, London's careful plotting of and for the mute Buck might suggest that allegory would be a more accurate critical category. Mark Seltzer has recently made a case for such allegorizing by wittily dubbing London and his animals "men in furs."[8] But it is *The Call of the Wild*'s very resistance to transparent allegory which is remarkable, since we continue to imagine London's hero as a dog despite all his complex mental attributes. London's surprise at his contemporaries' assessment of his tale as an allegorical treatment of the human jungle may very well have been feigned.[9] Yet the fact remains that he does manage to make Buck look and act like a dog-hero until the very end of his narrative, even if at times Buck's nature as a beast needs to be reinforced by simile. When we read at one point that Buck enters camp so exhausted that he "lay down like a dead dog" (28), we are forced to make a dizzying series of negotiations that prevent us from resting easily in either human or animal realms.

How does London manage this effect? First, Buck is powerfully gendered in ways which cut across species lines, so that his maleness allows London to hold onto the animal as a "he." Second, and more complex, is the pattern London sets up in the first half of the narrative whereby Buck is put into a situation not in his control, then invested with a human mentality and morality to evaluate the situation (to give it *values* that coincide with London's own as narrator), and then represented as reacting to that situation by way of "instinct," a kind of black-box biological explanation that enables London to maintain the doctrinaire survival-of-the-fittest logic that ostensibly drives his plot.

I say "ostensibly" because there are really *two* plots driving London and Buck, and the far more important one (neglected by most critics who have been blinded by the text's dogmatic Darwinism) has more to do with values than instincts. The central paradox informing the narrative is that Buck must learn to be wild. Wildness in this book is not simply a state of nature to be gained or regained by a reversion to type, as the naturalist plot of primordial atavism would have it. Attaining wildness entails disciplined education, technical and moral, a distinction collapsed by the representation of work/writing. The famous "call" that Buck heeds thus has more to do with a vocation or professional calling than some mysterious instinctual pull towards nature. *White Fang*, the companion piece to *The Call* that seems to reverse direction by tracing the progressive taming of a wild wolf, is in this sense less a sequel to Buck's experience than a simple replaying, making explicit what is more covert in the earlier tale. To name Buck's training a "paradox" may be a bit generous, however, since more accurately there is a massive set of contradictions about Buck at the heart of the narrative, which moves in two seemingly opposite directions at once: towards nature from culture (the standard naturalist plot of decivilization), and towards self-transcendence, a more troubled but also more passionate movement that cannot be fully contained by the conventional naturalist model.[10]

For one thing, the naturalist plot of decline depends on some clear demarcation between nature and culture, however much a continuum exists between the two poles (as London argued in his reply to Roosevelt). Without some such clear distinction, no linear plotting can make much sense.[11] London seeks to keep the two distinct yet linked by three types of mediation, all centering on the vague notion of the "primitive" (12): the "law of club and fang" (15); the representations of Buck's inherited racial memory during which the dog reverts back to a prior savage state of attendance on now "hairy" (41) masters (examples of London's "men in furs"); and the curious introduction at a key juncture late in the narrative of a tribe of Indians, the Yeehats, who presumably operate somewhere in between Buck's world and Jack's. In the case of all three of these mediations, London draws attention to the very "faking" of nature that he would gloss over. By eliding club and fang under a single primitive "law," for example, London confuses the means of human instrumentality with its end, in this case training via negative conditioning, as a behaviorist might say. While it might be argued that both club and fang seek to establish dominance, London carefully insists that the man in the red sweater beats Buck to gain obedience, not conciliation. Similarly, why in the world should masters, hairy or otherwise, be dwelling in Buck's racial unconscious, as if human mastery over nature were somehow natural in itself?[12] Such questions point to the cross purposes at work throughout the novel as London tries to negotiate or navigate his dog-hero between the animal world and the human.

Taking stock of his hero at one point during his narration, London himself captures this doubleness quite nicely: "His development (or retrogression) was rapid" (22). Trying to have it both ways and still avoid commitment (by using "or" rather than "and"), this assertion follows close on the heels of a more extended bit of commentary, a good example of London's self-conscious protesting or of the narrative clogging he pointed out in his defense: "This first theft [of a slice of bacon] marked Buck as fit to survive in the hostile Northland environment. It marked his adaptability, his capacity to adjust himself to changing conditions. . . . It marked, further, the decay or going to

pieces of his moral nature, a vain thing and a handicap in the ruthless struggle for existence. . . . Not that Buck reasoned it out. He was fit, that was all,
and unconsciously he accommodated himself to the new mode of life" (21).
Unlike a typical character in a realist novel who possesses a highly developed
moral nature subject to decay, Buck is a dog from the start; London's fixation
on morality immediately triggers his anxiety about Buck's reasoning, or lack
thereof. Precisely when moral considerations are introduced, considerations
well beyond the issue of Buck's adaptation to his environment, London feels
compelled to register some sharp distinction between beasts and men even
as he goes on to insist that "civilized" Buck "could have died for a moral
consideration, say the defence of Judge Miller's riding-whip" (21). That Buck
"civilized" begins life under a judge is no coincidence, especially since it would
presumably be the judge's "moral consideration" and not the dog's own that
would motivate the animal's defense of the whip—a symbolically resonant
piece of his master's private property that functions simply as a sleeker version
of the club which disciplined Buck in the wild.

Focusing on the programmatic aspects of the story's naturalism, Charles
Walcutt surmises that London makes his hero a dog because "if Buck were
a man there would have to be some kind of ethical responsibility."[13] The
decay of his "moral nature" can thus be tossed aside without the reader losing
respect for Buck. But London is *obsessed* with his dog-hero's moral nature and
the question of "justice" (13); it is precisely Buck's sense of value, especially
his own worth in the eyes of others, that wins our respect, as a quick glance at
the early chapters demonstrates. The clear succession of emotions that Buck
experiences in the opening scenes, cast as a captivity narrative, is quite striking: "a fine pride in himself" ruling over the Judge's ranch as a "sated aristo-
crat" (6); followed by "rage" once his "quiet dignity" (7) is repeatedly affronted
by his captors; followed by "obey[ing]" (12) the law of the club (obedience
explicitly distinguished from "conciliat[ion]"); followed by feeling "ashamed"
(anger turned inward by others' disapproval) when laughed at by "onlookers"
(14); followed by "hat[red]" (16) of his immediately recognized rival Spitz.

Pride, dignity, anger, obedience, shame, and hatred, culminating in
"imagination," a "quality that made for greatness" (35) which finally allows
Buck, perversely enough, to kill his dreaded rival. Animals may have "a logic
of feelings,"[14] but their emotions are not necessarily structured by a coherent narrative leading to self-fulfillment. Buck's character develops along the
lines of a traditional nineteenth-century bildungsroman, in which identity is
a process of becoming via moral education: a portrait of the dog as a young
artist, if you will. Compared to the figures inhabiting, say, Crane's *Maggie* or
Norris's *McTeague*, Buck is not only smarter but has a clearer sense of right
and wrong—is *more* human.

Such acquired humanity casts doubt on a key argument underpinning June Howard's ideological analysis of naturalism. Persuasively demonstrating how the genre's preoccupations with force and fate serve to express middle-class Americans' fear of proletarianization, Howard insists that turn-of-the-century naturalist texts starkly polarize the categories of helpless brute (character) and privileged spectator (narrator). But Buck's education, via work, suggests that for London these class-based antinomies are not as rigid and absolute as Howard suggests, that an upwardly mobile working dog (and his narrator double) can be a humanized beast without necessarily becoming a brute.[15]

Learning his many "lessons" (12, 15, 18), knowing his proper place, disciplining his body, and struggling for approval, Buck fulfills a higher calling. This calling has less to do with the wild than with the dignity of labor. *The Call of the Wild* thus strictly follows the dictates of the bildungsroman plot in that the transformation of nature by work leads to self-transformation, leads up from slavery to freedom. For Buck and Jack, work becomes the source of identity, the means to make a name for themselves. Functioning as a path to self-transcendence, labor in London's narrative thus carries enormous philosophical import—Hegelian import, to be more specific.

Hegel, not Darwin, offers the common ground for the oft-noted split in London between his Marxist-socialist side and his preoccupation with Nietzschean supermen. Marking a division between nature and culture, Hegel posits self-consciousness as separating humans from animals—the same sort of crucial distinction that London evoked in his response to Roosevelt's "nature-faking" charge. Self-consciousness can be gained, according to Hegel, only when animal desire negates itself, that is, moves outside itself to desire something beyond self-preservation. Beyond the instinct to survive there is the desire for desire itself, manifested as a quest for recognition. This struggle to be valued, to be found worthy by others, demands the dominance of one man over another; hence the origins of a master/slave dialectic whereby the conquered slave ("having subordinated his human desire for recognition to the biological desire to preserve his life"), by working, becomes master over nature, and in doing so frees himself from nature as well as from himself, from his nature as a slave. Quite simply, work humanizes, freeing the slave from the master, whose idleness fixes his identity as static.[16]

This may be a fairy tale, as Marx's historical-materialist explanation for subjugation makes clear, but it is Buck and Jack's fairy tale, nonetheless. Dog recognition, not dog cognition, becomes the central issue in the narrative, first in terms of how Buck is evaluated by humans, then by his fellow dogs, and finally and most problematically by his lover and master John Thornton. Initially valued strictly for his potential for work (size, strength, and ferocity),

Buck's "worth" is measured in human terms by money in the marketplace (as in many slave narratives) and by other means of rational calculation: "'One in ten t'ousand,'" his new owner Perrault "comment[s] mentally" (13) during the moment of exchange.

Once Buck enters into social relations with his fellow sledmates—also the precise moment he enters into work—his "worth" takes on a new meaning. As London introduces his crew of dogs, he gives them each a distinct personality—introspective, appeasing, fair, wise, lazy, and so on—largely in relation to how Buck values them and how they value Buck. More to the point, perhaps, is how intimately these evaluations become linked to Buck's "calling," his learning to pull the sled with his mates. The ability of Solleks, for example, to "command respect" is limited by his lack of "apparent ambition," until Buck later sees him at work with his partner Dave and "learns" to value their "even more vital ambition" (17). Like the two "new kind of men" (13) driving them, Dave and Solleks on the job suddenly become "new dogs, utterly transformed by the harness. All passiveness and unconcern had dropped from them. . . . The toil of the traces seemed the supreme expression of their being, and all that they lived for and the only thing in which they took delight" (19).

When London tries to give this Hegelian self-transcendence via labor a Darwinian slant, the results are quite peculiar, as in the famous "ecstasy" passage that London inserts right before he has Buck kill Spitz:

> There is an ecstasy that marks the summit of life, and beyond which life cannot rise. And such is the paradox of living, this ecstasy comes when one is most alive, and it comes as a complete forgetfulness that one is alive. This ecstasy, this forgetfulness of living, comes to the artist, caught up and out of himself in a sheet of flame; it comes to the soldier, war-mad on a stricken field and refusing quarter; and it came to Buck, leading the pack, sounding the old wolf-cry, straining after the food [a rabbit] that was alive and that fled swiftly before him through the moonlight. He was sounding the deeps of his nature, and the parts of his nature that were deeper than he, going back into the Womb of Time. (33–34)

Buck's ambition to lead the pack, otherwise always expressed in terms of work, suddenly is manifested in hunting a wild rabbit in the heat of the kill. London matches this primal thirst for blood by moving spatially inward ("deeps") and temporally backward ("Womb of Time"), so that transcendence can be converted into, or *repressed* as, instinct—"the deeps of his nature." But the first half of the passage undermines the latter, insofar as London needs to keep reminding us of our forgetfulness, illustrated by examples of an artist and soldier at work producing, or at least willfully act-ing—not unconsciously tearing into raw flesh.

In an interesting footnote to his influential reading of Hegel, Alexandre Kojève remarks that animals do have "techniques" (a spider's web), but that for the world to change "essentially" and become "human," work must real-ize a "project" or, as he says a bit later, be activated by an "idea."[17] Through a regimen of service and self-discipline, Buck's "idea" embodied in work is to become the leader of the pack by conquering "the disciplining" (17) Spitz, his rival for mastery. Once he defeats Spitz in this "war" (29) and gains from both dogs and humans the recognition and respect for which he has struggled, then what is there left for him to do? Since Buck is part of Jack's plot, since London in the act of narrating is himself working *for* Buck, we are able to see glimpses of a larger project informing the labor of narration. That idea or ambition is writing itself.

* * *

Buck has been associated with writing from the very first sentence of the story: "Buck did not read the newspapers, or he would have known that trouble was brewing" (5). This is certainly a strange way to introduce a dog-hero, making Buck's (not) reading at first seem a matter of mere preference rather than possibility (using "did" vs. "could") and thereby establishing a kind of subjectivity via a reference to the materiality of writing, which fades away by the end of this opening paragraph. Before it is clearly fixed that his protagonist is an animal, London's little joke here is to make us imagine the act of reading, and then immediately negate that reading by embodying the reader as a dog. The result is a trace or residue leaving the possibility of Buck's comprehension of print, as if the news of the Klondike gold strike that occasions his subsequent captivity is somehow available to him. Literal-izing in this way the operations of the unconscious, London positions Buck midway between a passive sign to be read and a reader of signs himself.[18]

The most important link between Buck and writing concerns his work itself, his toiling in the traces to deliver letters. It is quite extraordinary, though hardly ever noticed by critics, that in a tale ostensibly devoted to represent-ing the howling blank frozen white wilderness of the Yukon both men and dogs serve a noble civilizing function, bringing mail to the remotest outposts of progress, "carrying word from the world" (40). Even more pointedly, these "new men," François and Perrault, act as official agents of the state, "couri-ers" carrying various "government" (Canadian) "despatches" (16, 19). It is the very "important" (19) and "urgent" (32) nature of these dispatches, moreover, which accounts for the urgency of London's own labor as writer, the need to get his message out, be recognized by others for his work, and make a name for himself. As in the case of Poe's purloined letter, we never see the contents of these important dispatches, for London's emphasis falls on the delivery of mail, how writing gets circulated, distributed, and published after it is initially composed. Toiling in the traces that leave their own marks on the white landscape, both Buck and Jack fulfill their calling.

In a long footnote to his discussion of London, Mark Seltzer anticipates my claim about the inscription of writing on landscape, only to reject such an interpretation by insisting that a mechanics of literary production under what he calls naturalism's "body–machine complex" forecloses such a "traditional" notion of writing as a means to self-identity.[19] Here Seltzer is implicitly interrogating the work of Walter Benn Michaels, who has brilliantly argued that for the naturalist writer self-possession via the work of writing entails a self-consumption leading to a thematics of writing that can neither be reduced to its material marks nor transcend its materiality, just as the writer's person is neither identical with body nor independent of it. Seeking to challenge Michaels's positing of self (and totalized market) as a closed circuit of exchange, Seltzer tends to overemphasize the role of technology in literary production, at least in the instance of London, whose understanding of writing is less mechanistic than organic, drawn from the animal realm, as Seltzer's own powerful reading of "men in furs" shows. As my reliance on Hegel indicates, I would argue that London in fact holds very traditional assumptions about work and writing; in response to Michaels's thesis, however, I will be making a case for London's modernity by suggesting how he understands that an author's circulated name can ultimately carry more weight than the production of marks themselves.

Working like a dog finally is not enough, then, and by implication neither is writing like one. Once Buck vanquishes Spitz to achieve his highest ambition as top dog, he is soon after sold (by "official orders," 40) to a new (nameless) master, also a mailman but not apparently a government courier. London's plotting here begins to grow less urgent. The disenchanting of work actually begins shortly before Buck becomes leader of the pack. In a long, self-conscious, overheated passage celebrating "that nameless, incomprehensible pride of the trail and trace" (30), London conflates Buck's "desire for mastery" (30) over Spitz with the pride that all these dogs take "in the toil to the last gasp," the "ordained order that dogs should work" (31). But for Buck to gain supremacy over the pack, he must *disrupt* work, must break down "discipline" (32) to "destroy the solidarity of the team" (32). Describing this "challenging [of Spitz's] authority" (32) in terms of an "open mutiny" (30) or "revolt" (32), London points to a gratification beyond work: "He [Buck] worked faithfully in the harness, for the toil had become a delight to him; yet it was a greater delight slyly to precipitate a fight amongst his mates and tangle the traces" (33). It is surely no coincidence that in the very next paragraph London allows Buck and his fellows to go off chasing that wild rabbit. Working gives way to hunting, an activity more akin to play or sport that celebrates blood lust (desire) more than eating for survival (need).

While London does his best to offer the spirit of defiance as a means of transcendence that surpasses discipline and servitude, Buck is finally no demonically driven Ahab, for the problem seems rather more mundane: sheer disgust and exhaustion with work itself. With Buck now at the lead, London suddenly remarks that "it was a monotonous life, operating with machine-like regularity. One day was very like another" (40). Pages later his last desperate effort to restore the nobility of work has precisely the opposite effect. In London's most extended treatment of another dog, something goes "wrong" with that wonderful worker Dave, who becomes "sick unto death" (43), suffering from a mysterious "inward hurt" (44) that would not go away despite his overwhelming "pride of trace and trail" (43). London settles this existential crisis as best he can, celebrating in reverent tones the fact that "a dog could break its heart through being denied the work that killed it" (44), and then finally putting Dave out of his misery with a pistol shot whose meaning Buck "knew" (44). So much for Hegel.

Speaking for Buck, why should Jack in the end also find that "his heart was not in the work" (50), even as this "heart" can still remain "unbreakable" (54)? A significant clue to the answer can be found in a curious little essay entitled "How I Became a Socialist" that London first published in March 1903, just as he was negotiating the book publication rights to *The Call of the Wild*.[20] The most productive and important year of his life, 1903 also saw, among other personal events, the publication of London's book *The People of the Abyss*, an account of his journalistic foray the previous summer into the East End of London, where he poignantly charted the conditions of the British underclass.[21] In both essay and book London's central metaphor for this underclass is an abyss or bottomless pit; what he makes clear in his essay is that "socialism" primarily serves simply to keep him from falling into such a pit. London begins autobiographically by remarking that as a young "MAN" he used to be "one of Nietzsche's *blond beasts*," "one of Nature's strong-armed noblemen" who proudly believed that "the dignity of labor was … the most impressive thing in the world." Associating such "orthodox bourgeois ethics" with "rampant individualism," he claims that this "joyous individualism" was "hammered out" of him as soon as he began to come in close contact with "what sociologists love to call the 'submerged tenth'"—the underclass that industrial capitalism uses up and discards. Conveniently forgetting his own (illegitimate) birth in the pit of the working-class, London ends his little story with an italicized vow strange enough to merit quoting in full: "*All my days I have worked hard with my body, and according to the number of days I have worked, by just that much am I nearer the bottom of the Pit. I shall climb out of the Pit, but not by the muscles of my body shall I climb out. I shall do no more hard work, and may God strike me dead if I do another day's hard work with my body more than I absolutely have to do*" (1119). This oath is remarkable for at least three reasons. First, in disavowing his own beginnings in the pit, London "confesses" that he is primarily motivated by the "terror" of join-ing the underclass. He expresses absolutely no solidarity, the working-class consciousness that Marx and Engels saw as necessary for revolution. Second, given his terror of the pit, work itself becomes terrifying; the goal is not to struggle to make work less alienating and thereby rehumanize it, but merely to "run away" and escape it altogether. Third, and perhaps most remarkable, London simply equates manual labor with "hard work." I take "hard" here also to mean "difficult," so that he is by implication suggesting that brain work would somehow necessarily be easy. But then trying actually to imag-ine his "reborn" life without such deadening hard work, London is forced to admit, "I was running around to find out what manner of thing I was," a state of being that he rather optimistically labels "socialist."

London's essay might have been more accurately titled "How I Became a Successful Author," for it carries enormous implications for my previous discussion of the presence of writing throughout *The Call of the Wild*. Ear-lier I emphasized the physicality of writing for both Buck and Jack: hauling the heavy letters inch by inch through a blank white wilderness. Writing's materiality thus renders nature immaterial. But London's distinction between hard work and easy work suggests a second more abstract notion of writing in which the author controls and manages the deployment of letters but does not actually carry them himself. In the scene of writing that informs the nar-ration up to this point, London is both slave, figured as Buck toiling in the traces, and *simultaneously* figured as master, the plotter who directs the course of the sled and the beasts he uses (buys and sells) to pull it. The writing mas-ter thus hopes to gain some control within a potentially degrading capitalist market. But once hard work is fundamentally called into question, starting with the death of the dog Dave, how can letters be moved at all? That is, how can writing be strictly easy? Commenting on Hegel, Kojève notes that the bourgeois worker under capitalism has no master but nonetheless freely accepts his enslavement by the idea of private property, of capital itself.[22] London turns this fear on its head by imagining "socialism" as a state of mas-tery without slavery, without any hard work, so that the writer is now free to roam in search of "what manner of thing" he has suddenly become. In the end

London is left looking for a kind of easy work to replace the hard work that he has given up.

Given this disenchanting of hard work and hard writing, London would seem to be abandoning his dog-hero's project for self-transcendence as well, so that it is difficult to imagine how Buck's education can proceed. With the sacrifice of Dave, the plot threatens to stop dead in its tracks. One clear possibility is to fall back on the Darwinian model of instinctual regression, which, we have seen, has so far consisted mainly in Buck and the other dogs chasing rabbits. I am perhaps being flippant here, since there are clearly key moments in the narrative when London powerfully evokes a sense of a "dominant primordial" (24)—manifested as "ancient song" (22–23), "wild fathers" (32), "blood-longing" (77), and so on—pulling the beast Buck back into his primitive past. But these passages are quite literally *lyric*, in that they are almost always detachable from the plot, neither closely following from prior events nor leading to others. The relationship between chasing rabbits and the "ecstasy of living," for example, is tenuous at best. Such ecstasy is powerful, in fact, precisely insofar as it can effectively escape London's plotting.

Powerful and dazzling, such intermittent evocations of nature most importantly keep Buck an animal and are therefore precisely the points of resistance that prevent the type of transparent allegorizing I earlier rejected but might now seem again to be bordering on: Hegel in furs. Insofar as London depends on his role as plotter deploying and delivering letters to give him his status as writing/publishing master, such ecstatic moments threaten to sever the ties between Jack and Buck. At the risk of slighting the dog's ostensible return to the wild, I want to pursue for the remainder of this essay the problem of authorial mastery—a growing concern for London that manifests itself in his partial disengagement from Buck the dog as a primary source of identity in the later stages of the novel and his increasing identification instead with human characters.

What remains for London then, before letting go of his plot, letting humans "pass out of Buck's life for good" (40), is to comment on the writing of the story itself through a series of cautionary tales with interesting consequences. Instead of development or reversion we get a kind of stasis or holding pattern, as London presents a pair of moral lessons about bad masters and good masters. This structure of alternating bad and good masters bears a close resemblance to many animal tales for children (such as *Black Beauty*), as well as to episodic slave narratives.[23] More important, from this point on in London's narrative, morality will no longer be rooted in Buck's nature, or even in his masters', as the plot begins to take on decidedly theological overtones.

First, the bad masters, an unlikely trio of husband, wife, and wife's brother. They appear on the scene immediately after London alludes to "congested mail" (46)—a striking homonym punning on the impasse in his plot and the thwarting of Buck's manhood. New "official orders" (46), from nowhere, suddenly demand the sale of the dogs, who are said to "count for little against dollars" (46). Up to this juncture in the narrative, Buck's continuity of identity depends on carrying letters, but Charles, Mercedes, and Hal are not couriers with urgent dispatches. What they are doing venturing through the North, in fact, remains to the end a "mystery of things that passes understanding" (46)—a New Testament echo (*Philippians* 4:7) that seems to refer as much to London's uncertainty about their motives as to Buck's uncertainty, just as the subsequent paragraph's narrative commentary—"a nice family party"—seems to capture Buck's ironic disgust as well as London's.

Here then is Buck and Jack's worst "nightmare" (53), toil without writing, toil without project, toil without meaning. Not only are their motives uncertain, but these new masters are technically incompetent to boot: "They were slack in all things, without order or discipline" (51). In the most prolonged departure from Buck as a center of consciousness for the narrative, London gives us an unsubtle satire about the dangers of domesticated irrational feminine disorganization (the sin of "dishes unwashed" mentioned twice). Confronted with an alien environment, the overcivilized family registers chaos, whereas the state of wildness clearly depends on strict regimentation, possible only through regulated work. Given the absence of such service, at once ennobling and enabling, nature can be represented only by negation: what it is not. The two men unwisely overburden the dogs, the family quarrels, Mercedes gives in to "the chaotic abandonment of hysteria" (57), and all three finally and foolishly fall through thin ice, taking with them all their dogs, except for the presciently stubborn Buck. A kind of providential punishment for their poor mastery, the "yawning hole" (58) that they leave in their downward plunge serves brilliantly to literalize London's fable of negative transcendence. Hal and Charles and Mercedes have truly become the people of the abyss.[24]

Once the bad masters drop out of the picture, we might expect Buck to respond immediately to the call of the wild. But before he can be free of all encumbrance he owes a debt of gratitude to his savior, John Thornton, a debt he will pay back in spectacular fashion. Entitled "For the Love of a Man," the John Thornton chapter seems totally out of place, contributing to neither Buck's working education nor his instinctual regression. The episode instead functions as a religious parable of sorts in which Love as a single unifying transcendental signifier is meant to subsume—in effect cancel out—both the dignity of labor and the law of club and fang. And what a love it is—"feverish and burning, that was adoration, that was madness" (60)—that emerges out of nowhere and strains, if not absolutely bursts, the boundaries of London's plot.

As the repetition of "adoration" makes clear, Buck's passion is religious and therefore presumably not a form of slavery; perhaps the dog-hero will find his true "calling" as a disciple. London seems to be working on the analogy that Buck is to other dogs as Thornton is to other men. Buck thus can meet his match only by worshipping a god, an "ideal master" (60). As perfect master, however, Thornton grants Buck an all too perfect freedom, letting him do nothing and consequently, in Hegelian terms, forcing him to be nothing. Even though Buck cannot overcome bad masters without some providential aid, at least his passive resistance to the family trio allows London to maintain his dignity. But dignity becomes a problem for both Jack and Buck once Love dissolves all such resistance, freeing them *from* work instead of freeing them *to* work. Trying to sustain an oxymoron (ideal mastery) by an imposed religious analogy (Christ incarnate), London ends up constantly operating at cross purposes, oscillating wildly, as Buck does, between elevating Thornton and ignoring him so that he can heed his call.

Thornton's progressive diminishment manifests itself in two connected ways: his odd assumption of various gender roles and his equally strange simulations of work. In keeping with his status as ideal master, he is initially figured as a benevolent father seeing to "the welfare of his [dogs] as if they were his own children" (60). The problem is that Buck is no ordinary pet but a special being, closer to his master, closer to humans (if other dogs are dogs), closer to a god (if other dogs are just human). Portraying the intense intimacy between Buck and Thornton, London is compelled to level the difference between man and beast, to make them share the same ontology. First London equalizes their respective powers of verbalization: the moment Thornton rescues Buck, he is said to utter "a cry that was inarticulate and more like the cry of an animal" (57); a few pages later Thornton sees Buck's "throat vibrant with unuttered sound" and gushes "God! you can all but speak!" (60). When letters disappear, "with the mail behind them" (42), sounds will have to do.[25] The communion between the two grows more problematic once London gives their mutual love a physical basis; in addition to Buck's religious "adoration" by way of his respectfully distant "gaze" (61), we are privy to a more corporeal sort of love play where the two males "embrace" (60) and caress each other until Buck's "heart would be shaken out of his body so great was its ecstasy" (60).

From god the father to male lover, Thornton more and more plays the part of wife, and a badly treated one at that. London first introduces Thornton in this chapter as "limping" (59) and home-bound, a condition that reinforces Buck's growing sense that his love for John "seemed to bespeak the soft civilizing influence" (61). In the wake of the bad masters satirized in the previous chapter, this influence is clearly feminine and domestic, "born of fire and roof" (61), and therefore to be avoided at all costs. Lest I seem unduly harsh about London's opinion of the feminine here, a brief review of the four "shes" in the novel should set things straight: 1) Curly, who is savagely ripped to shreds by the other dogs and thereby conveniently becomes the source for Buck's hatred of his (male) rival Spitz; 2) Dolly, "who had never been conspicuous for anything" (28) but suddenly goes "mad" (dog hysteria?); 3) Mercedes, who "nurse[s] the grievance of sex" (53); and 4) finally Skeet, Thornton's "little Irish setter" who "as a mother cat" nurtures the wounded Buck, whose "dying condition" prevents him from "resent[ing] her first advances" (59). He is mercifully saved from the threat of a same species, heterosexual relationship only by finding a higher love in John. Once Buck starts to feel the pull of the primitive, then Thornton's domesticity becomes a decided nuisance, as the dog more and more takes to hanging out with his wolf companions, "sleep[ing] out at night, staying away from camp for days at a time" (76). Prone to sentiment and tears (56, 70, etc.), the wronged Thornton can meanwhile only wait at home for the straying, unfaithful lover now "seized" by "irresistible impulses" and "wild yearnings" (74). A vulnerable victim finally unable to defend himself in the wilderness, Thornton is anything but lord and master by the time he meets his fate.

Thornton's "calling" as a worker follows a similar trajectory. Like the previous bad masters, this good one does not deliver letters. Nor does he do much of anything else. A wounded god, he lazily waits, as Buck does, to heal himself. Love of course is the means of healing for both, but this mutual passion soon begins to resemble suspiciously a curious kind of work whereby Buck must prove himself all over again. Their love turns into a series of perverse tests (edited from the story's first serialized version); while defending his master against a legendary desperado and then saving his life (tests #2 and #3) can be explained in terms of Buck's gratitude, a payback, how do we explain Thornton's command that Buck jump off a cliff (test #1)? Fortunately not carried out, this "experiment," which Thornton calls "splendid" and "terrible" (63), may strike the reader as not simply "thoughtless" (63), but downright sadistic, especially once we imagine (as we have been invited to do) that Thornton and Buck are human lovers.

Perhaps even stranger is Buck's final test (#4), yet another "heroic" "exploit" (66) that explicitly takes the place of work. Boasting like a proud lover about the prowess of a mate, Thornton borrows money to bet heavily on Buck's ability to haul a heavy sled against a famous "Bonanza King" (67). Here the hard work of Buck as sled dog delivering letters is mocked as a kind of "free play" (69), especially when Thornton actually wins the bet, which is made for hard cold cash ($1600), rationally calculated, not for honor or dignity. By means of an empty gesture (the sled goes nowhere and is filled with dummy weight), Buck's worth is converted into market speculation. We have come full circle, since London's plot is initially triggered by betting as well: recall that Buck is sold in the first place to pay off the lottery debts of the Mexican gardener whose "faith in a [gambling] system . . . made his damnation certain" (7). For both Manuel and Thornton, Buck equals bucks.

"When Buck earned sixteen hundred dollars in five minutes for John Thornton, he made it possible for his master to pay off certain debts and to journey with his partners into the East after a fabled lost mine, the history of which was as old as the history of the country" (71). So begins the final chapter of the novel. Given the narrative's prior emphasis on work, the devastating irony of that term "earned" is a bit troubling, as is the perfunctory nature of the rest of the rambling sentence, as if Jack simply wanted to get his story over and done with, swiftly make his *own* Big Buck, and go home to enjoy the fruits of his labor now that those "certain debts" have been discharged, thanks to Buck's five minutes of love.

Here the autobiographical and vocational dimensions of the narrative become most apparent, for John Thornton clearly doubles for John "Jack/Buck" London, as the recent excellent edition of London's letters helps us to see. Linked by London's obsessive concern with the material conditions of his craft, the writer's life and fiction tend to merge. The $1600 that Thornton wins by gambling on Buck, for example, almost matches the $1800 that London sought (and got) as an advance from his book publisher, Macmillan Company. In an extraordinary pair of letters to his editor George Brett (dated 21 Nov. and 11 Dec. 1902), London lays out an absurdly ambitious scheme to write six books in *one* year, plans filled with word counts, dollar amounts, debts, profits, market values, financial risk, and production timetables—the stuff of rationalized capitalism. London at this time (like Thornton) enjoyed "doing credit on a larger and Napoleonic scale" (letter to Cloudsley Johns, 27 Jan. 1903), in effect trading on the promise of his name.[26]

Yet despite London's heavy investment in the writer's market, the heroic deeds that Buck has performed for his master suggest another sort of economy operating in the end, an economy that depends less on Buck's work as a mail carrier and more on the spreading of his "reputation" and "name . . . through every camp in Alaska" (64). That is, the sign that Buck finally produces for himself is not the mark of writing but the mark of fame—a difference that entails a shift in the narration from work to adventure. Heroism suddenly leads to a "wander[ing]" (72) search for that "fabled lost mine"; although the Lost Cabin remains a mystery, Thornton's fabulous get-rich-quick scheme of course succeeds; London briefly narrates how "like giants they toiled, days flashing on the heels of days like dreams as they heaped the treasure up" (73), while "there was nothing for the dogs to do" (73). This self-conscious modulation into legendary fame and fortune looks forward to Buck's eventual apotheosis as immortal "Ghost Dog" (85), a kind of concluding emblem for London's career aspirations as a writer.

If this novel is an allegory at all, it should be read as an uncanny anticipation of the course of London's professional "calling," his great popularity—starting with the publication of *The Call of the Wild*!—as well as his subsequent struggles to maintain and manage his success in the literary marketplace. Striking it rich, London's revenge on his public is not to stop writing, as Buck stops working; instead London becomes driven, drives himself, to write more, to write about himself, about his own fame, over and over again until he eventually breaks down. In this respect his fate as a writer closely resembles the fate of the workaholic dog Dave, whose chronic "inward hurt"—"something wrong inside" (43) that cannot be fixed—ultimately kills him. Imagining the career of Buck, London traces a more satisfying path. As totemic leader of the (wolf) pack, Buck is obliged only to "muse" (86) dutifully at the final resting place of his beloved master, nature's own altar of the dead, sometimes bringing his wolf companions along with him. In this way we are reminded that from start to finish, Buck has never lost touch with civilization.

During the novel's concluding wish-fulfillment in permanent celebrity, London makes one final effort to sustain some moral tension in his narration by representing Buck as torn between his allegiance to his adored human master and his increasing kinship with his wild wolf "brother" (76, 85). But this growing conflict within Buck is conveniently cut short by the sudden introduction of a band of Indians—the Yeehats—who render the question of the dog-hero's moral choice moot. Without a "trace" (83), Thornton's exit from the narrative as sacrificial victim is as surprising as his entrance as perfect master and lover. While Thornton's abrupt departure allows London and his readers to return at the end to Buck as a primary source of identification, such a reaffirmation of the wild's call exacts its own price.

A kind of parody of the primal horde of sons whom Freud imagines as slaying the father in *Totem and Taboo*, the Yeehats kill Thornton and his mining partners while Buck is off enacting his nature as primordial beast by tenaciously stalking a "great" (81) old bull moose. London thus offers an astonishing series of displaced murders: while Buck is killing the moose, primitive Indians kill his white master; the Indians are in turn killed in a rage by Buck, who must revenge the master's murder "because of his great love"—a love, London adds, through which Buck "lost his head" (82). With "reason" (82) now conflated with instinct and "passion" (82) located in civilization, London's booby-trapped naturalism finally explodes, forcing us to scramble for other sorts of supernatural explanations. Having tasted men's blood, "the noblest game of all" (83), the dog-hero is finally free to become Top Wolf, leaving both the human world *and* nature behind for good (or at least until he reappears as "White Fang").

The difficulty is that in Freud's version of this sacred myth Buck (the son) must kill Thornton (the father) directly, in order to resolve the problem of authority by and for himself. Nietzsche's retelling similarly demands that Buck (the human) directly kill Thornton (the god). But by introducing middlemen, London chooses *for* his animal-hero a weaker resolution that would seem to beg the fundamental question of Buck's moral transcendence. The savage Yeehats in effect allow the dog to remain civilized, thereby draining Thornton's sacrificial murder of its sacred power. Although he may be a "Fiend incarnate" (82, see also 10, 37, 58, etc.) when it comes to killing the Indians, Buck doesn't appear man enough to do the real job himself.

Buck's masculinity has been a central issue throughout the entire narrative—on Judge Miller's ranch, in captivity, at work transmitting messages, and finally as a "killer" in the wild (77). In the end, then, perhaps Buck's true calling depends less on whom he murders than on the spectacular way he does it, given the crucial transformation in the novel from toiling in the traces to instant success during the staged sled pull. London's progressive disenchantment with work in the story registers the growing fear felt by many turn-of-the-century American men that the market, increasingly abstract and rationalized, could no longer offer the grounds to define manhood, particularly in terms of those ideals of self-reliance, diligence, and mastery at the heart of nineteenth-century liberal individualism.[27] Once the workplace diminishes in significance in the new century, masculinity threatens to become primarily a performance or pose displayed for its own sake, like the theatrical shows of passion which characterize the Thornton–Buck relation ("as you love me, Buck"), and the dog-hero's equally melodramatic final conquests of bull moose, Yeehats, and wolf pack (just prior to which Buck is said to stand "motionless like a statue" [84]). Buck's toil as a letter carrier gains him respect and recognition, but his intense killing ultimately grants him the iconographic status of Ghost Dog, an awe-inspiring totem far more powerful and lasting than civilized man's paler version, fame.

Seeking to test manhood in noneconomic arenas (the wilderness, war, sports), turn-of-the-century Americans such as Teddy Roosevelt struggled to combat a mounting spiritual crisis in masculinity by trying to naturalize dominance. In one of his earlier excursions into literary criticism, an 1892 review of Kipling and other writers praising war, Roosevelt remarks that "every man who has in him any real power of joy in battle knows that he feels it when the wolf begins to rise in his heart."[28] London's own wolfish quest for power is a bit more subtle than Roosevelt's, less patently "homocentric," to reinvoke the terms of his counterattack against TR's "nature-faking" charge. Taking Roosevelt's glib metaphor literally, London in his naturalist masterpiece imagines himself becoming—through captivity, delivering letters, and ritual slaying— the very male-creature Roosevelt can only superficially conceive of as a man in wolf's clothing. In contrast to TR's imposed metaphoric pretense, Buck under London's direction does work as a highly charged cultural carrier. For this reason *The Call of the Wild* continues to merit our attention. Simultaneously on extravagant display and buried deep, like a bone, within his animal-hero, Jack London's mail manages to affirm his own public calling—to make his bold mark for all to admire.

NOTES

1. Edward B. Clark, "Roosevelt on the Nature-Fakirs," *Everybody's Magazine*, June 1907, 770–74; supplemented by Theodore Roosevelt, "Nature Fakers," *Everybody's Magazine*, September 1907, 427–30. Calling Roosevelt a member of the Ananias Club (a liar), London replies in "The Other Animals," *Collier's*, 5 September 1908, 10–11, 25–26. See also Roosevelt's letter to his friend and fellow target of attack John Burroughs (12 March 1907), as well as his subsequent angry response to *Collier's* editor Mark Sullivan (9 September 1908) in *The Letters of Theodore Roosevelt*, 8 vols., ed. Eltinge E. Morison (Cambridge: Harvard Univ. Press, 1952), 5:617, and 6:1220–23. Roosevelt ends his letter to Sullivan by saying that he would no sooner enter into a serious controversy with London about his fiction than he would seriously engage the writer's views on social or political reform.

2. There has been a recent rash of popular accounts of this still controversial issue. See, for example, Marian Stamp Dawkins, *Through Our Eyes Only: The Search for Animal Consciousness* (Oxford: Freeman, 1993); Elizabeth Marshall Thomas, *The Hidden Life of Dogs* (Boston: Houghton Mifflin, 1993); Vicki Hearne, *Animal Happiness* (New York: HarperCollins, 1994); and Stanley Coren, *The Intelligence of Dogs: Canine Consciousness and Capabilities* (New York: Free Press, 1994). For a highly original view interrogating the way modern science has historically construed the relation between humans and animals, see Donna Haraway, *Primate Visions* (New York: Routledge, 1989).

3. Cited in C. C. Walcutt, *American Literary Naturalism: A Divided Stream* (Minneapolis: Univ. of Minnesota Press, 1956), 96–97.

4. Christopher Wilson, *The Labor of Words: Literary Professionalism in the Progressive Era* (Athens: Univ. of Georgia Press, 1985).

5. Walter Bern Michaels, *The Gold Standard and the Logic of Naturalism: American Literature at the Turn of the Century* (Berkeley: Univ. of California Press, 1987), particularly the introduction ("The Writer's Mark"); Michael Fried, *Realism, Writing, Disfiguration: On Thomas Eakins and Stephen Crane* (Chicago: Univ. of Chicago Press, 1987); Mark Seltzer, *Bodies and Machines* (New York: Routledge, 1992). A fourth important recent study of American naturalism is worth noting here: Lee Mitchell, *Determined Fictions* (New York: Columbia Univ. Press, 1989). Mitchell's discussion is at once conceptually broad and methodologically narrow.

The strong claims he makes for naturalism's radical undermining of conventional philosophical assumptions about personal agency and identity are based on a series of rather traditional stylistic analyses (examining syntactical repetition, for example) that focus in isolation on individual naturalist texts (a single short story in the case of Jack London).

6. Jack London, *The Call of the Wild*, in *Novels and Stories* (New York: Library of America, 1982). Subsequent page citations are from this edition.

7. The comparison to Kipling and Seton is frequently made, but often in rather general terms. See for instance James Lundquist, *Jack London* (New York: Ungar, 1987), 100.

8. *Bodies and Machines* (New York: Routledge, 1992), 166.

9. London claimed, with perhaps some real justification, that he was "unconscious" while writing the novel. See Joan London, *Jack London and His Times* (New York: Doubleday, 1939; reprint, Seattle: Univ. of Washington Press, 1968), 252.

10. Christopher Wilson briefly notes the same paradox, but perhaps too optimistically claims that the two plots work in "counterpoint." See *The Labor of Words*, 104.

11. For an important discussion of naturalist plotting, see June Howard, *Form and History in American Literary Naturalism* (Chapel Hill: Univ. of North Carolina Press, 1985). Emphasizing the binary opposition between nature and culture, Howard admits that such antinomies are "unstable" (53) in London's *White Fang*. Yet she goes on to rely on a structuralist model (Greimas's semiotic rectangle) in a way that too readily accepts London's constructed oppositions as givens.

12. In a footnote Walcutt briefly ponders the same sorts of questions, which he leaves unanswered. See Walcutt, *American Literary Naturalism*, 311 n. 22. It might be argued that Social Darwinism works precisely to naturalize the notion of human mastery, but Buck's atavistic reversion to savagery would more logically remove him from the human realm entirely.

13. Ibid., 106.

14. This striking phrase is used in a series of 1880s essays on the relation between human and animal psychology written by George John Romanes, a professor and popular explicator of Darwin whom London cites in his *Collier's* reply to Roosevelt. See George Romanes, *Essays* (London: Longmans, Green and Co., 1897), 71, 75.

15. June Howard, *Form and History in American Literary Naturalism*, chapters 3 and 4.

16. This brief summary of Hegel's master/slave dialectic is based on Alexandre Kojève, *Introduction To the Reading of Hegel* (Ithaca: Cornell Univ. Press, 1980), 3–70. The quoted passage can be found on page 42. By seeing Hegel (as read by Kojève) as the source for London's Nietzsche and Marx, I am not making claims for direct influence; while to my knowledge Hegel is not mentioned by London in his letters or essays, Hegel powerfully informs American literature's conceptual foundations, as a recent collection of essays has suggested. See *Theorizing American Literature: Hegel, the Sign, and History*, ed. Bainard Cowan and Joseph G. Kronick (Baton Rouge: Louisiana State Univ. Press, 1991). For a fleeting allusion to Hegel pertaining to London, see Joan D. Hedrick, *Solitary Comrade: Jack London and His Work* (Chapel Hill: Univ. of North Carolina Press, 1982), 138.

17. Kojève, *Introduction to the Reading of Hegel*, 52, 64.

18. London's joke is even more pointed in the serialized version of the story, which was first published in *The Saturday Evening Post*, a mass-circulation magazine with a large format closely resembling a daily newspaper. We thus begin the story by reading the news of Buck reading the news.

19. *Bodies and Machines*, 224–25.

20. Jack London, "How I Became a Socialist," *Novels and Social Writings* (New York: Library of America, 1982), 1117–20.

21. London started writing *The Call of the Wild* sometime during December 1902 and was finished by the middle of January 1903; the novel was serialized the following summer (beginning June 1903) in *The Saturday Evening Post*. In addition to writing the novel and the essay on socialism and preparing *The People of the Abyss* for publication the following fall, London during this remarkably productive period also published the novel *The Kempton-Wace Letters* (published anonymously, co-authored by Anna Strunsky), bought the sloop *Spray* to sail around the San Francisco Bay, began writing *The Sea-Wolf* (virtually completed by the end of the year), separated from his wife and children, and fell in love with his future wife, Charmian Kittredge.

22. Kojève, *Introduction to the Reading of Hegel*, 65. Basing class distinctions on the difference between mental and manual labor, London uncharacteristically falls prey to a vulgar Marxism, an argument all the more surprising since his essay was published by the prominent socialist editor John Spargo, who in other contexts criticized such confused and unscientific thinking. See Daniel T. Rodgers, *The Work Ethic in Industrial America, 1850–1920* (Chicago: Univ. of Chicago Press, 1978), 219–20, 229. Presumably securing London's famous name for the socialist cause was more important than the depth of his analysis.

23. See Charles N. Watson, *The Novels of Jack London* (Madison: Univ. of Wisconsin Press, 1983), 36, for a brief comparison between *Black Beauty* and *The Call of the Wild*. Watson also offers an interesting comparison between *The Call* and *White Fang* that shows the structural similarities between these two plots, despite the latter's ostensible reversal of direction (85). For the suggestion that *The Call of the Wild* functions in some ways as a slave narrative, I am indebted to my student Benjamin Diamond.

24. Earlier in the narrative Spitz falls through the ice, leaving Buck on the slippery edge, straining in a panic with Dave and François to pull Spitz back and thereby save themselves, since they are all linked to the sled by the traces (27–28). The writing of these two fictional passages about the abyss is clearly informed by London's terror of falling into the social Pit.

25. Later in the narrative, in describing Buck's newfound "pride in himself" as a killer, London remarks that this pride "advertised itself . . . as plain as speech" in Buck's physical swagger (77). The shift from pride in work to pride in killing is thus matched by the shift from writing to public (advertised) speaking.

26. Like Thornton, London was wounded, maimed during the writing of *The Call of the Wild* in a manner almost too good to be true: "A heavy box of books fell on me, striking me in a vital place" (letter to Anna Strunsky dated 20 January 1903). Here the hazards of a career in letters take on a physical dimension. See *The Letters of Jack London*, ed. Earle Labor, Robert C. Leitz III, and I. Milo Shepard (Stanford: Stanford Univ. Press, 1988), Vol. 1.

27. There are numerous historical analyses of this crisis. See, for example, Joe L. Dubbert, "Progressivism and the Masculinity Crisis," in *The American Man*,

ed. Elizabeth H. Pleck and Joseph H. Pleck (Englewood Cliffs, NJ.: Prentice-Hall, 1980), 303–20; T. J. Jackson Lears, *No Place of Grace: Anti-modernism and the Transformation of American Culture, 1880–1920* (New York: Pantheon, 1981); and E. Anthony Rotundo, *American Manhood* (New York: Basic Books, 1993), chapters 10 and 11.

28. Theodore Roosevelt, "A Colonial Survival," in *The Works of Theodore Roosevelt* (New York: Scribner's, 1926), 12:306.

ANDREW J. FURER

"Zone-Conquerors" and "White Devils": The Contradictions of Race in the Works of Jack London

"A symposium on Anglo-Saxon supremacy!" exclaims Frona Welse, in Jack London's first novel, expecting to find her views affirmed by her fellow "zone-conquerors," London's term for what he saw as the Anglo-Saxon's tendency to conquer the peoples of the various climatic "zones"—the Arctic, the tropics:

> We are a race of doers and fighters, of globe-encirclers and zone-conquerors. We toil and struggle . . . no matter how hopeless it may be. . . . Will the Indian, the Negro, or the Mongol ever conquer the Teuton? Surely not! The Indian has persistence without variability; if he does not modify he dies, if he does try to modify he dies anyway. The Negro has adaptability, but he is servile and must be led. As for the Chinese, they are permanent. All that the other races are not, the Anglo-Saxon, or Teuton if you please, is. All that the other races have not, the Teuton has. What race is to rise up and overwhelm us?[1]

Although Frona seems an unwavering champion of white supremacy, her creator's views of this question are far from constant. In several of London's Pacific tales, for example, he valorizes Chinese and Hawaiian ancestry: Ah

From *Rereading Jack London*, edited by Leonard Cassuto and Jeanne Campbell Reesman, pp. 158–71, 261–65. Copyright © 1996 by the Board of Trustees of the Leland Stanford Junior University.

Chun "perceived little details that not one man in a thousand ever noticed. . . .
He did not . . . figure in politics, nor play at revolutions, but he forecast
events more clearly than the men who engineered them. . . . Ah Chun was a
power. . . . [He] was a moral paragon and an honest business man."[2] Stephen
Knight, "athlete. . . . [was] a bronzed god of the sea . . . [with] a quarter-strain
of tropic sunshine in his veins. . . . [Dorothy Sambrooke] . . . pleasur[ed] in
the memory of the grace of his magnificent body, of his splendid shoulders,
of the power in him."[3]

Much of London's writing deals with conflicts between the individual and the collective, and his views of race constitute a substantial part of
the drama of such struggles. London is unquestionably attracted to ideals
of white superiority; he created a series of Anglo-Saxon supermen, such as
Wolf Larsen of *The Sea-Wolf*. *Martin Eden*—one of the few of London's 50
books that his publisher, Macmillan, kept in print for most of the twentieth
century—contains several passages of blatantly anti-Semitic material.[4] From
one perspective, such racist views could be construed as a response to social
and biographical pressures. London was six years old when the first Chinese Exclusion Act was passed, in response to Californians' fears of having
to compete in a depressed job market with thousands of Chinese laborers; he
was in his mid-twenties when the Exclusion Act was indefinitely extended.
Biographer Andrew Sinclair notes that London's mother told her son that he
was from a distinguished American family, that he was "better than the Irish
and Italians and other people who had recently come to the United States,"
and that he had "a birthright which he must defend from them."[5]

London, however, frequently subverts those views in works such as
"Chun Ah Chun," "Koolau the Leper" (1909/1912), and "The Mexican"
(1911/1913). These works and other similarly antiracist pieces, a significant
part of his later work, have been overshadowed by his widely anthologized
Alaskan fiction and such well-known novels as *The Call of the Wild*, *The Sea-
Wolf*, and *Martin Eden*. As a result, the richness and complexity of this powerful and prolific author have yet to be fully recognized, especially in regard to
his racial views.[6] London overcomes his pro–Anglo-Saxon bias only where
the environment is less harsh and, more important, wherever he finds or creates non-white protagonists of superb courage and power. Their exceptional
qualities—whether of body, mind, or spirit—allow the author, without anxiety, to elevate the so-called inferior races (what he elsewhere calls "mongrels"
or "scrubs") to a cultural position equal to or even superior to that of whites.
London introduces a "man [or woman] on horseback" who is not a "blond
beast."

Critics, both favorably and unfavorably inclined toward London, have
found his views on ethnicity to be essentially racist. Among writers with a

negative view of London, William E. Cain is especially harsh. In a review of London's collected letters, Cain notes London's "contempt for black, brown and Jewish people" and "his reiterated racist . . . ballyhoo" and asserts that "it would be misleading . . . to imply that in his fictional and nonfictional work London overcomes the disfiguring ideas that he espouses in his letters."[7] In his recent book, *Bodies and Machines* (1992), the New Historicist Mark Seltzer remarks upon "the terroristic . . . racial violence" in London's stories of "the great white . . . North."[8]

Even such sympathetic London scholars as Earle Labor, Charles N. Watson, Jr., and Susan Nuernberg acknowledge the powerful appeal that racism had for him, noting that he reflected racial views then highly popular, such as those of Benjamin Kidd.[9] Labor emphasizes "the sad historical fact . . . that many of the leading 'scientific' thinkers of [London's] age embraced various doctrines of white supremacy and that millions of decent Americans bought books which blatantly preached 'racial egotism' and taught their readers to 'despise the lesser breeds.'"[10] Watson states that "notions of Anglo-Saxon supremacy were in their heyday, and London's fiction often reflected—and perhaps contributed to—their advance."[11] Nuernberg concurs in this view, adding that at the time, America needed to justify its imperialist policies.[12] Most London scholars interested in this issue also are careful to point out instances of antiracism in his work, noting that his views in this area, as in so many others, are "a bundle of contradictions" (Labor, "London's Pacific World," 214). However, there have as yet been few attempts to link his paradoxical views of Anglo-Saxon superiority, miscegenation, and the non-white races.

Before discussing the ways London's antiracist works powerfully valorize the non-white races and ridicule ideas of white supremacy and racial "purity," I must first comment briefly on several works in which he seems most deeply invested in his Anglo-Saxon supremacist views, so we can understand the strong appeal that white supremacy held for him. In *A Daughter of the Snows*, he has Frona and other characters sing frequently the praise of the Anglo-Saxon. Frona gives the lengthy lecture, "We are a race of doers and fighters . . ."; Captain Alexander proclaims that "the white man is the greatest and best breed in the world" (85). Frona's suitor, Vance Corliss, exclaims, "These battlers of frost and fighters of hunger! I can understand how the dominant races have come down out of the north to empire. Strong to venture, strong to endure, with infinite faith and infinite patience, is it to be wondered at?" (146).

He and Frona then take turns reciting verses from Norse sagas: London calls her a "furred Valkyrie" (ironically, Frona is of Celtic origin). Corliss, London writes, feels "strangely at one with the white-skinned, yellow-haired giants of the younger world" (148) and sees the "sea-flung Northmen, great-muscled, deep-chested, sprung from the elements, men of sword and sweep, marauders and scourgers of the warm southlands! The din of twenty centuries of battle was roaring in his ear, and the clamor for return to type strong upon him" (148). Here we see one of the main appeals for London of Anglo-Saxon supremacist ideology: a positive form of atavism, a clean and pure reversion to type. A return to the life of such "sea-flung Northmen" is very different from the brutish, degrading, criminal, or diseased kinds of atavism he portrays in *Before Adam* (1906) or "When the World Was Young" (1910/1913)—the protagonist of the later story, though the author describes him as an "early Teuton," behaves more like a caveman.[13] The degraded type of atavism is a common obsession among naturalists; Frank Norris, for example, wrote two novels, *Vandover and the Brute* (1914) and *McTeague* (1899), about such degeneration.[14] In *A Daughter of the Snows*, London champions an Anglo-Saxon supremacy based on a strife-filled heritage. He nonetheless represents the race not only as the "smiter and destroyer" of the ancient world but also as its "builder and law-giver" (147), morally superior to other races, untainted by deception and deviousness, doing its sins "openly, in the clear sight of God" (201). Its origins are also free of the taint of urban civilization, since the race comes from the sparsely populated North: "This is the world, and we know of fact that there are very few people in it, else there could not be so much ice and sea and sky" (261).[15] Celebrating the Anglo-Saxon gives London a way to bless the lower forces—the "brute"—in the human being, rather than condemn them.

In this view, he departs from the evolutionary theory of one of his mentors, Herbert Spencer: "out of the lower stages of civilisation higher ones can emerge, only as there diminishes [the] pursuit of . . . revenge and re-revenge which the code we inherit from the savage insists on."[16] Spencerian social evolution "incorporates the concept of definite stages; progress is from the 'militant' to the 'industrial' type of society."[17] The same year that London published *A Daughter of the Snows*, Spencer stigmatized contemporary militaristic sentiments as signs of degeneration and "re-barbarisation"; he sees an unfortunate atavistic return of "barbaric . . . ideas and sentiments, and an unceasing culture of blood-thirst."[18] London, however, at least in his first novel, finds that under certain harsh conditions (such as those obtaining in the Arctic), the recrudescence of Anglo-Saxon "barbaric" traits is a desirable phenomenon.

Even in this work, one of the most racist of London's novels, there are signs of antiracism. Gregory St. Vincent, who initially "correspond[s] well to [Frona's] idealized natural man and favorite racial type" (133), turns out to be a liar and a moral and physical coward. Furthermore, one Indian character wonders to herself "that the accident of white skin or swart made master or servant as the case may be" (191). There are at least the beginnings here of a dialogue about simplistic assumptions of racial superiority.

London's late novel *The Mutiny of the Elsinore* includes another such instance of antiracist material in an otherwise virulently racist work, a hint at thin spots in the armor of Anglo-Saxonism. *Elsinore*'s narrator repeatedly trumpets the glories of the blond races: "Yes, I am a perishing blond . . . , and I sit in the high place and bend the stupid ones to my will; and I am a lover, loving a royal woman of my own . . . breed, and together we occupy, and shall occupy, the high place of government and command until our kind perishes from the earth."[19]

Alongside such passages, however, the novel features episodes depicting an extremely courageous and capable non-white character. Initially a servant, he is later shown to be a master of men, at least in combat. The narrator, in the midst of a fierce battle with the mutineers, suddenly sees his Japanese valet, Wada, "charg[e] like a buffalo, jab [a mutineer] . . . in the chest with the spear he had made and thrust [the mutineer] . . . back and down" (*Elsinore*, 339). Despite the narrator's representation of him as merely a servant, Wada emerges as a figure of power, as effective in battle as any white man aboard the *Elsinore*.

Just as there are hints of egalitarian views in some of London's more racist works, there are also several places, especially in his journalism, where he praises a non-white race yet reveals an anxious xenophobia. In much of his war and personal correspondence on the Russo-Japanese War, and in articles such as "The Yellow Peril" (September 25, 1904), written later on similar topics, London praises the Japanese highly: "as to the quietness, strictness and orderliness of Japanese soldiers it is very hard to find any equals in the world."[20] Furthermore, he states, they are "a race of warriors and their infantry is all that infantry could possibly be."[21] Comments such as these, however, eventually lead to fear and disquietude: "The Japanese are so made that nothing short of annihilation can stop them," he writes while watching their successful attack on the Russians at Antung, their men "streaming darkly" to the attack. Later that day, London sees some Russian prisoners:

> I caught myself gasping. A choking sensation was in my throat. . . .
> I found myself suddenly and sharply aware that I was an alien
> amongst these brown men who peered through the window with
> me. And I felt myself strangely at one with those other men behind
> the window—felt that my place was there inside with them in their
> captivity, rather than outside in freedom amongst aliens.[22]

He also praises the Chinese for being as adept economically as the Japanese are militarily. The threat of efficiency and overwhelming numbers represented by the cooperation of the two races makes him anxious:

> Four hundred million indefatigable workers (deft, intelligent, and unafraid to die), aroused and rejuvenescent, managed and guided by forty-five million additional human beings who are splendid fighting animals, scientific and modern, constitute that menace to the Western world which has been well named the "Yellow Peril."[23]

Although he admires these two races, en masse they frighten him. Their valorization of the collectivity and devaluation of the individual seems both inhuman and immoral to him. He declares, "The Japanese is not an individualist. He has developed national consciousness instead of moral consciousness. . . . The honor of the individual, per se, does not exist. . . . Spiritual agonizing is unknown to him" ("Yellow Peril," 349). Joan London, in her biography of her father, notes that upon his return to San Francisco from the war, his socialist comrades had to listen to him curse "the entire yellow race in the most outrageous terms" and declare that "I am first of all a white man and only then a Socialist."[24]

The fear of the horde (vigorously painted in chapter 23 of *The Iron Heel* in general terms and in "The Unparalleled Invasion" [1910/1914] in specifically anti-Asian terms) is a powerful one. In his short story collection *The House of Pride*, however, fear of the Yellow Peril almost entirely disappears. When London gives Asian and other non-white characters individuality accompanied by exceptional ability, his anxiety dissolves into admiration, and he begins to see numerous ways in which people of color are superior to Anglo-Saxons. Indeed, in contrast to the racial views in his journalism and in such fictions as *A Daughter of the Snows*, the title, *The House of Pride*, alone is provocative: the title story illustrates the pernicious pride and racism of a white character, but the only justified and morally correct pride expressed in all these stories is that of Polynesians, mixed breeds, and Asians.

Chun Ah Chun is one of those who has much to be proud of—he is a philosopher merchant-king, who arrived in Hawaii as a mere peasant: "He was essentially a philosopher, and whether as coolie, or multi-millionaire and master of many men, his poise of soul was the same" ("Chun Ah Chun," 152). In his daily life, he solves "problems such as are given to few men to consider" (153). Ah Chun is a Chinese Cowperwood or Rockefeller, but with none of the character flaws of these fictional and nonfictional titans of finance. After only three years working on a sugar plantation, Ah Chun starts his own business, having discovered, as had London early in life, "that men did not become rich from the labor of their own hands" (154). Ah Chun then goes into the labor-importing business and many others, amassing a fortune. He is a man of great vision, imagining Honolulu as a modern city with electricity while it was still a primitive sand-blasted settlement set on a coral reef.

His career totally refutes Frona's contention that the Chinese are unable to adapt to new conditions. Further, Ah Chun eventually comes to preside over "an atmosphere of culture and refinement second to none in all the islands" (169). No one in Hawaii is too proud to visit him. Later, when he leaves Hawaii to retire to his native land, first landing at Macao, Ah Chun encounters racism at the finest hotel there—the clerk tells him that Chinese are not permitted, and the manager scornfully insults him. He leaves and then returns after two hours, having bought the hotel. During the months following, he increases the hotel's earnings from 3 percent to 30 percent, meriting a description that London elsewhere (see, for example, "The Inevitable White Man" [1910/1911]) reserves for the white race: he is "inevitable," a man of power and mastery, not unlike many of London's dominant Anglo-Saxon protagonists, such as Wolf Larsen or Martin Eden: "Chun Ah Chun had long exercised the power of a king" (186).

This story includes not only a non-white master of men but also a description of the benefits of miscegenation, a practice London criticized harshly in his Mexican War correspondence, among other places.[25] Ah Chun marries a woman who is part Anglo-Saxon and part Polynesian, with the former predominating. They produce fifteen sons and daughters, among whom, the author writes, "the blend of races was excellent" (161). These offspring are very beautiful, precisely because of their mixed blood. Their father "had furnished the groundwork upon which had been traced the blended pattern of the races. He had furnished the slim-boned Chinese frame, upon which had been builded the delicacies and subtleties of Saxon, Latin, and Polynesian flesh" (162). They are also intelligent and well educated: one son goes to Harvard and Oxford, two others go to Yale, and the girls go to Mills, Vassar, Wellesley, and Bryn Mawr. It is true that his high-spirited family causes him many problems, but they are still exceptional progeny. Further, London uses them to show that white society's adherence to ideals of racial purity is itself impure and up for sale. When Ah Chun has trouble marrying his daughters to highly placed whites, he begins to give his daughters large dowries: "That will fetch that Captain Higginson and his high family along with him" (179), he says. Suddenly, his daughters are regarded as eligible.

This is not the only story in which London praises the fruits of miscegenation. In "The Seed of McCoy" (1909/1911) a descendant of the *Bounty* mutineers and Pitcairn Islanders saves a ship with a cargo of burning wheat and pacifies its frantic and mutinous crew through his Christlike calm and mastery of seamanship. McCoy, great-grandson of the McCoy of the *Bounty*, replies to an aggressive inquiry into his identity by stating, "'I am the chief magistrate,' . . . in a voice that was still the softest and gentlest imaginable."[26] The captain and the mate of the burning ship, the *Pyrenees*, initially judge McCoy by his shabby clothes: "that this barefooted beach-comber could possess any such high-sounding dignity was inconceivable" ("The Seed of McCoy," 265). They soon find, however, that this mixed-breed is able to ease the fears of the crew and revive their weary souls. "[McCoy's] smile was a caress, an embrace that surrounded the tired mate and sought to draw him into the quietude and rest of McCoy's tranquil soul" (264). Later, when the crew seems ready to mutiny because of the ship's delayed landfall, "their faces convulsed and animal-like with rage" (270), McCoy's presence, "the surety and calm that seemed to radiate from him, . . . had its effect" (274): "His personality spoke more eloquently than any word he could utter. It was an alchemy of soul . . . profoundly deep—a mysterious emanation of the spirit, seductive, sweetly humble, and terribly imperious. It was illumination in the dark crypts of their souls, a compulsion of purity and gentleness vastly greater than that which resided in the shining, death-spitting revolvers of the officers" (307). Ironically, McCoy is the product of a clash between white men and Tahitians. The whites, McCoy says, were "terrible men . . . they were very wicked. God had hidden His face from them" (310). The Tahitians' response to these men was little better: "The mutineers . . . killed all of the native men. The [native] women helped. And the natives killed each other. Everybody killed everybody" (310). Yet the mixing of the blood of these two races produces the Christlike McCoy. In this story, London allows that while racial strife brings out the worst in humanity, miscegenation can bring out the best.

It is likely that London's views of the benefits of hybridization, as expressed in many of the *House of Pride* stories, were influenced by his friendship with horticulturalist and philosopher Luther Burbank. In June 1906, Burbank wrote to London:

> The splendid book "White Fang" received and I thank you *most* heartily for this esteemed token of your friendship. We shall all enjoy reading it very much and if it is as good or better than the "Call of the Wild" and some others that you have given us it will have great educational value to say nothing of its value as a most absorbing story. We will tap it this evening and if I don't get up for breakfast tomorrow morning it will be your fault I am sure. Here goes my best wishes for you and Charmian for a prosperous and happy voyage.[27]

According to Ken Kraft and Pat Kraft, London, a "repeat visitor" to Burbank's ranch, "loyally planted Burbank cactus on his ranch for stock feed, in the teeth of warnings from University of California agricultural experts."[28] London's biographer Clarice Stasz, in addition to remarking upon London and Burbank's friendship, notes the resemblance of Darrell Standing, the "agriculturist" protagonist of London's science fiction novel, *The Star Rover*, to Burbank. In *The Training of the Human Plant* (1907), written during the year that he first met London, Burbank emphasizes "the opportunity now presented in the United States for observing and, if we are wise, aiding in what I think it is fair to say is the grandest opportunity ever presented of developing the finest race the world has ever known out of the mingling of races brought here by immigration."[29] He also claims that "by the crossings of types, strength . . . intellectuality . . . [and] moral force" have "been secured" (12). Another passage from Burbank suggests an additional source of hybridization's attraction for London:

> Just as the plant breeder . . . notices sudden changes and breaks . . .
> when he joins two or more plants of diverse type from widely separated quarters of the globe,—sometimes merging [a] . . . wild strain
> with one that, long *over-civilized, has largely lost virility,*—and just
> as he finds among the descendants a plant which is likely to be
> stronger and better than either ancestor, so may we notice constant
> breaks and changes and modifications going on about us in this
> vast combination of races, and so may we hope for a far stronger
> and better race . . . a magnificent race, far superior to any preceding
> it. (9, emphasis added)

In Burbank's account, hybridization can be the basis for biological social reform, a kind of racial therapy to rid *fin de siècle* Americans of "over-civilization." In "Chun Ah Chun," London champions a Chinese titan of finance, but he also, as noted above, praises the great beauty and ability of Ah Chun's children, who are "one thirty-second Polynesian, one-sixteenth Italian, one-sixteenth Portuguese, one-half Chinese, and eleven thirty-seconds English" (160).

London was writing about the benefits of interbreeding, however, even before he met Burbank. In "The Story of Jees Uck" (1902/1904), the protagonist of which is an Alaskan "mixed-breed," London states, "What with the vagrant blood in her and the heritage compounded of many races, Jees Uck developed a wonderful young beauty."[30] In addition, she displays a capacity for decisive and powerful action; seeing Amos, the man who has tried to poison her husband, Neil Bonner, she "spring[s] like a tigress upon Amos and with splendid suppleness and strength bend[s] his body back across her knee" ("Jees Uck," 257). London represents her as a counterirritant to the jaded Anglo-Saxon race: she constitutes "an immeasurable sum of pleasurable surprise to the overcivilized man that had . . . [caught] her up. . . . In Jees Uck he found the youth of the world—the youth and the strength and the joy" (262–63).

London also found people of superb strength and endurance among the natives of Hawaii. "Koolau the Leper," in the same collection as "Chun Ah Chun," provides a capable non-white character who achieves personal triumph in the face of overwhelming odds and a significant disability, while poignantly illustrating the evils that whites had brought into the South Seas. The story begins with Koolau detailing the whites' injustice to the Polynesian lepers. He says to his followers, "Because we are sick they take away our liberty. We have obeyed the law. We have done no wrong. And yet they would put us in prison. Molokai is a prison. . . . It is the will of the white men who rule the land. . . . They came like lambs, speaking softly. . . . To-day all the islands are theirs."[31] Here London casts a negative light on Roosevelt's ideal of "speaking softly and carrying a big stick." Koolau and his people are thrice-wronged, as Kapalei, a former jurist, who is now "a hunted rat" (56), indicates:

> The sickness is not ours. We have not sinned. The [white] men who preached the word of God and the word of Rum brought the sickness with the coolie slaves who work the stolen land. I have been a judge. I know the law and the justice, and I say to you it is unjust to steal a man's land, to make that man sick with the Chinese sickness, and then to put that man in prison for life. (57)

London emphasizes the moral superiority of the Polynesians by giving this speech to a man of high rank and great insight who has been brought low by the greed, hypocrisy, and arrogant callousness of Anglo-Saxon invaders.

Earle Labor, in his essay "Jack London's Pacific World," sees this story as "representative of London's attitude toward the underdog" (211), but although Koolau and his people are undoubtedly persecuted, Koolau, despite his deformity, is a figure of mastery and power. He had been a "lusty, whole-bodied youth" (90), and now, an expert marksman, he feels "a . . . prod of pride" because more than 100 men, London writes, "with war guns and rifles, police and soldiers . . . came for him, and he was only one man, a crippled wreck of a man at that. They offered a thousand dollars for him, dead or alive" (78). As Labor states, "He is indomitable spiritually—a . . . magnificent rebel" (211). Koolau holds a mountain passage against the soldiers for two days, then during a parley, he announces with pride and dignity: "I am a free man. . . . I have done no wrong. All I ask is to be left alone. I have lived free, and I shall die free. I will never give myself up" ("Koolau," 86). The soldiers pursue him for six weeks, but his "sure rifle" and his wilderness abilities frustrate their efforts, so they abandon the attempt and leave the Kalalau Valley to him. Ironically, he thus regains some of the stolen lands, and lives for two more years.

James I. McClintock states that Koolau "salvages his individual dignity but dies according to 'the law' enforced by whites."[32] The ending of the story, however, seems to undermine this interpretation. As Koolau lies dying of his disease, having escaped the white "law" in the Kalalau Valley, he recalls his youth and his mastery over nature, and, London writes, "his last thought is of his Mauser, and he pressed it against his chest with his folded, fingerless hands" ("Koolau," 91). His last act is that of a warrior. It is true that his people have deserted him, but this shows that—in London's view—in spite of a dark skin, and a disease seemingly emblematic of degeneration, Koolau overcomes the Nietzschean "man on horseback," whose virtues are beyond race.

In 1908, while recuperating in Australia from bowel surgery and malaria, which had caused him to give up his *Snark* voyage, London accepted an assignment from the *New York Herald* to cover the world championship heavy weight bout between Tommy Burns and Jack Johnson. Early in his article on the fight, London argues for race solidarity, seeming to align himself with the dominant racial politics of the day, which assumed that white would and should cleave to white, black to black, and so on: "Personally I was with Burns all the way. He was a white man, and so am I. Naturally I wanted to see the white man win. Put the case to Johnson and ask him if he were the spectator at a fight between a white man and a black man which he would like to see win. Johnson's black skin will dictate a desire parallel to the one dictated by my white skin."[33] London goes on, however, to give Johnson his due: "Because a white man wishes a white man to win, this should not prevent him from giving absolute credit to the best man, even when that best man was black. All hail to Johnson" (146). Despite feelings of racial solidarity, London does not stint his praise for Johnson: "What . . . [won] on Saturday was bigness, coolness, quickness, cleverness, and vast physical superiority" (146). Racial stereotypes are absent from London's presentation of a "superior mind in a superior body" figure that he so admires, one who in this case happens to be black.[34] Indeed, given his portrait of the "inevitable white man" in other texts, the language London uses to compare Burns and Johnson is striking. The fight, he says, "had all the seeming of a playful Ethiopian at loggerheads with a small and futile white man, of a grown man cuffing a naughty child, of a monologue by one Johnson, who made noise with his fist like a lullaby, tucking one Burns into his little crib in Sleepy Hollow" (147).[35] In London's account, the only thing Johnson does wrong is that he does not knock Burns out when he has the chance.[36] The author, for all his early protestations about identifying with the white man here, seems in his egotism to identify with Johnson, who is clearly an exceptional individual and a master of men. Johnson was "superb. He was impregnable . . . as inaccessible as Mont Blanc" (148), a rather ironic simile. An August 18, 1911, interview in the *Medford Sun* bears the headline, "Prefers Jack Johnson's belt to the Crown of King George; Jack London Admires Fighters." The piece quotes London as declaring, "I would rather be heavyweight champion of the world . . . than King of England, or President of the United States, or Kaiser of Germany."[37]

London also covered Johnson's fight against James Jeffries, "the Great White Hope." The racial issues at this Reno fight were even more explicit than in the Burns contest. As Richard Bankes says, the promoter Tex Richard advertised the fight as "the ultimate test of racial superiority" (*Stories of Boxing*, 151). As a result, several hundred men roamed the streets of Reno, threatening to kill Johnson if he won. Interestingly, in London's early articles on the fight (he was to write one each day for the ten days preceding the fight, as well as an article about the fight itself), he inverts the era's stereotypical opposition of civilized white man and savage black man—he declared that Johnson's abilities were those of a scientific boxer while Jeffries' were those of a primitive fighter: "Jeff is a fighter, Johnson is a boxer. Jeff has the temperament of a fighter. Old mother nature in him is still red of fang and claw. He is more a Germanic tribesman and warrior of two thousand years ago than a civilized man of the twentieth century" ("No. 2" [June 24, 1910], 157).[38] Johnson also appears to be more sophisticated intellectually than Jeffries. The latter is a silent fighter; on the other hand, Johnson displays "genuine wit, keen-cutting and laughter provoking" ("No. 5" [June 27, 1910], 165). He reveals "positive genius" in placing his blows during a fight. Like London's other supermen—Ernest Everhard and Martin Eden, for example—Johnson combines a powerful, creative mind and a superb body.[39] If Martin is laborer as artist and intellectual, Johnson is boxer as artist and intellectual: "[Johnson] is a marvel of sensitiveness, sensibility and perceptibility. He has a perfect mechanism of mind and body. His mind works like chain lightning and his body obeys with equal swiftness" ("Jeffries–Johnson Fight" [July 4, 1910], 182).

It is not only among Asians, Polynesians, and blacks that London discovers masters, but among the "breeds" (as he calls them) of Mexico as well. In "The Mexican," Felipe Rivera has the spiritual indomitability and the physiological power of London's Anglo-Saxon heroes: he has a "deep chest," tough-fibered flesh, an "instantaneousness of the cell explosions of the muscles, [and] . . . fineness of the nerves that wired every part of him into a splendid fighting mechanism."[40] Furthermore, London is careful to note that "Indian blood, as well as Spanish, was in his veins" (261). Rivera, like Koolau, is a tragic figure—a sympathetic fellow revolutionist says, "He hates all people. . . . He is alone . . . lonely" (251). Nonetheless, he is admirable both in his strength and his ideals: he is a boxer who fights for money to help fund a socialist revolution in Mexico. Those in his revolutionary cell, the junta, are unaware of how Rivera gets money to bring them, but they are well aware of his force and dedication: "To me he is power—he is the wild wolf,—the striking rattlesnake," says one. To another, "He is the Revolution incarnate. . . . He is the flame and spirit of it, the insatiable cry for vengeance" (251).

McClintock states that Rivera is "that mysterious, inevitable, telic power that goes beyond intellectual commitment, even beyond patriotic emotion" (*White Logic*, 129). Unlike the whites in the fight game, he boxes not just for money, but for a glorious ideal and for the welfare of others. London states, "Danny Ward fought for money, and for the easy ways of life that money would bring. But the things Rivera fought for burned in his brain" (269). This, along with his exceptional muscular powers, makes him triumphant. Although he has an often unprepossessing exterior, he displays the melding of superior spirit and superior body, which London so worships in his Anglo-Saxon heroes—Elam Harnish, for example.[41]

In Rivera's ultimate fight—upon which depend $5,000 and the guns necessary to start the revolution—he finds that "all Gringos were against him, even the referee" (278), who counts long seconds when his opponent is down and short seconds when Rivera is. Through his strength and quick intelligence and his keen senses ("Rivera's ears were a cat's, desert-trained"), however, he triumphs over the whites' conspiracy of unfairness. (London refers to Rivera's handlers, who are white strangers, as "scrubs," a phrase he uses elsewhere as a derogatory term for mixed breeds.) Although his opponent is "the coming champion" and is helped by "the many ways of cheating in this game of the Gringos" (289), such as muttering vile racist insults to Rivera during the fight, Rivera is something much more, an "Übermensch": although only a boy of eighteen, "he had gone through such vastly greater heats that this collective passion of ten thousand throats, rising surge on surge, was to his brain no more than the velvet cool of a summer twilight" (288). Furthermore, like Ernest Everhard in *The Iron Heel*, he is a superman who is nonetheless devoted to the cause of the masses: "resplendent and glorious, [Rivera] saw the great, red Revolution sweeping across his land. . . . He was the guns. He was the Revolution. He fought for all Mexico" (282). After he has won the bout, "the Revolution could go on" (290). The skinny, dark mixed-breed is a far cry from the "blond beasts" of much of London's power-worshiping fiction, but this superior individual fighting for the people combines the two attributes London valued most: individual mastery and dedication to the socialist cause.

London's attraction to supermen and women of his own race is widely known. As I have tried to show here, however, he recognizes that exceptional individuals exist among other races, and he champions such figures as well. Indeed, his final, unfinished novel, *Cherry*, displays one of the most accomplished of his female characters, a young Japanese woman who combines the best of her Asian heritage with an excellent Western upbringing. She is "a finished creation of many a million years, a jewel of the quick, a selected culmination, a last biological and aesthetic word of womanhood" (1).[42] Cherry is also a born linguist and a scholar: "only a scholar could trip her while at the same time running the equal risk of being tripped by her" (14). Although London seems to use her to argue against miscegenation, and to make a case for racial purity as the way for each culture to produce its best citizens, the fact that intellectually and culturally she is a product of Hawaii's polyglot society subverts this view.

London's sympathy for the underdog is well known. Nonetheless, it is precisely his admiration for the spiritual and physical power to be found among those whom popular opinion of his day held to be inferior that persists through all the contradictions of his racial views. Many of these supermen and superwomen tend to emphasize, in their distinction, the benefits of self-culture and argue for a model of success that emphasizes differentiation rather than subordination to the greater social good. Characteristically, London often ignored such implications of his own views and valorized the collective over the individual. In 1916, London wrote to resign from the Socialist Party, claiming that it had lost its revolutionary fire. In this letter, in perhaps his final words on the race issue, questions of power and courage are inextricably linked to those of race and class: "If races and classes cannot rise up and by their own strength of brain and brawn, wrest from the world liberty, freedom and independence, they never in time can come to these royal possessions."[43]

Notes

1. Jack London, *A Daughter of the Snows* (New York: Grosset and Dunlap, 1902), 83. These racial views are echoed in some of London's early letters: "The negro races, the mongrel races, the slavish races, the unprogressive races, are of bad blood—that is, of blood which is not qualified to permit them to successfully survive the selection by which the fittest survive" (London to Cloudsley Johns, June 1899, in Earle Labor, Robert C. Leitz III and I. Milo Shepard, eds., *The Letters of Jack London*, 3 vols. [Stanford, Calif.: Stanford University Press, 1988], 1: 87).

2. London, "Chun Ah Chun," in *The House of Pride and Other Tales of Hawaii* (New York: Macmillan, 1912), 154, 156, 169. This story was initially published in

Woman's Magazine 21 (1910). Dates accompanying short story titles in the text are of initial magazine publication. I use these earlier dates, rather than dates of initial book publication, to emphasize that London's antiracist views are not contained within one narrow segment of his career.

3. London, "Aloha Oe," in *The House of Pride*, 131–32, 142–43, 144.

4. See, for example, the description of the Oakland socialist, "a clever few," with "stooped and narrow shoulders," who "stood forth representative of the whole miserable mass of weaklings and inefficients," in chapter 38 of the novel (London, *Martin Eden*, in Donald Pizer, ed., *Jack London: Novels and Social Writings* [New York: The Library of America, 1982], 854).

5. Sinclair, *Jack: A Biography of Jack London* (New York: Harper and Row, 1977), 4.

6. Nineteen of London's works were novels. He worked in nearly every genre, including drama, socialist manifesto, sports journalism, and travel narrative. His subjects include: agriculture, alcoholism, astral projection, big business, ecology, economics, gold-hunting, penal reform, political corruption, prizefighting, seafaring, socialism, war, and wildlife. There are some recent signs that more of his works are being given attention. Jeanne Campbell Reesman has noted that "in his later period in particular (though even here, not without exception), his tendency is toward portraying native peoples of non–Anglo-Saxon background not only sympathetically but as morally superior to Anglo-Saxons" (Introduction to "A Symposium on Jack London," *American Literary Realism* 24 [1992]: 4).

7. Cain, "Socialism, Power, and the Fate of Style: Jack London in His Letters," *American Literary History* 3 (1991): 604–5.

8. Seltzer, *Bodies and Machines* (New York: Routledge, 1992), 223 n. 35.

9. Benjamin Kidd (1858–1916), English civil servant, popular philosopher, and ardent Spencerian, was the author of *Social Evolution* (1894). The book brought him instant fame—within six years of its publication it had been translated into eight languages. Kidd's social philosophy, a simplistic application of the Darwinian concept of natural selection to social evolution, glorified the Anglo-Saxon contribution to history and divided humanity into stronger and weaker races.

10. Labor, "Jack London's Pacific World," in Jacqueline Tavernier-Courbin, ed., *Critical Essays on Jack London* (Boston: G. K. Hall, 1983), 214.

11. Watson, *The Novels of Jack London: A Reappraisal* (Madison: University of Wisconsin Press, 1983), 200.

12. See Nuernberg, "The Call of Kind: Race in Jack London's Fiction" (Ph.D. diss., University of Massachusetts, 1990).

13. London, "When the World was Young," in *The Night-Born* (New York: Century, 1913), 84. It is especially, if not exclusively, in the Arctic that this reversion can remain pure, as is evident by the contrast between the fate of atavistic whites there and those in Melanesia. See "Mauki" (1909/1912).

14. Although *Vandover* was not published until twelve years after Norris's death, it seems to have been written during his year (1894–95) as a special student at Harvard. See James D. Hart, ed., *A Novelist in the Making: Frank Norris* (Cambridge: Harvard University Press, 1970), 43–57.

15. Corliss says to Colonel Trethaway, "But it is the living strenuously that holds you," and then implies that "living strenuously" is not only "Frona's philosophy" (220) but that of any right-thinking Anglo-Saxon Alaskan.

16. Spencer, *The Study of Sociology* (London: Kegan, Paul, Trench, 1873), 199. London owned or borrowed dozens of Spencer's works; as David Mike Hamilton notes, "Herbert Spencer's work was part of the bedrock of London's philosophy" (*"The Tools of My Trade": The Annotated Books in Jack London's Library* [Seattle: University of Washington Press, 1986], 256). There are references to Spencer in almost all of London's novels.

17. David Wiltshire, *The Social and Political Thought of Herbert Spencer* (Oxford: Oxford University Press, 1978), 247.

18. Spencer, *Facts and Comments* (New York: D. Appleton, 1902), 133. (London's annotated copy of this work is at the Huntington Library.) These comments reflect Spencer's negative view of the Naval and Military Exhibition of 1901, which was in part a commemoration of the Great Exhibition of 1851. Spencer, in line with his view that the same laws govern the evolution of bodies and societies, and following his theory of "equilibration," states that societies are either evolving or degenerating; they never stand still.

19. London, *The Mutiny of the Elsinore* (Honolulu: Mutual Publishing, 1987), 337. This novel was serialized as *The Sea Gangsters* in *Hearst's Magazine* from November 1913 to August 1914.

20. London to Charmian Kittredge, Mar. 4, 1904, *Letters*, 1: 415.

21. London, [Description of army in Korea], in King Hendricks and Irving Shepard, eds., *Jack London Reports: War Correspondence, Sports Articles, and Miscellaneous Writings* (New York: Doubleday, 1970), 13, 42.

22. London, "Give Battle to Retard Enemy," in Hendricks and Shepard, *Jack London Reports*, 103, 106.

23. London, "The Yellow Peril," in Hendricks and Shepard, *Jack London Reports*, 347.

24. Joan London, *Jack London and His Times: An Unconventional Biography* (New York: Doubleday, 1939), 284.

25. See, for example, "The Trouble Makers of Mexico" (June 13, 1914), in Hendricks and Shepard, *Jack London Reports*. Writing of the *mestizos*, London declares, "They are what the mixed breed always is. . . . They are neither white men nor Indians. . . . They possess all the vices of their various commingled bloods and none of the virtues" (177). In the course of this article, London manages a backhanded compliment to Mexico's Indian population (or at least its male half), even as he condemns the country's "mixed-breeds": "[The half-breeds] are child-minded and ignoble-purposed; The stern stuff of manhood, as we understand manhood, is not in them. This stern stuff is in the pure-blooded Indians, however" (180).

26. London, "The Seed of McCoy," in *South Sea Tales*, intro. A. Grove Day (Honolulu: Mutual Publishing Paperback Series, 1985), 262.

27. Burbank to London, June 2, 1906, Jack London Collection, Henry E. Huntington Library. (The first communication between the two appears to have occurred the previous fall, when London wrote to Burbank requesting "a tip as to any kinds of exceptionally good fruits and grapes for me to plant" [London to Burbank, Oct. 7, 1905, Sonoma County Library].) I am not the first to propose the connection between London and Burbank's views of hybridization. Clarice Stasz makes a similar point in chapter 8 of her *American Dreamers: Charmian and Jack London* (New York: St. Martin's Press, 1988). In his autobiography, Burbank describes London as a "big healthy boy with a taste for serious things, but never cynical, never bitter, always good-humored and humorous, as I saw him, and with fingers and

heart equally sensitive when he was in my gardens" (Burbank [with Wilbur Hall], *The Harvest of Years* [Boston: Houghton Mifflin, 1927], 225). A photograph of London and Burbank examining spineless cacti is included in Russ Kingman, *A Pictorial Life of Jack London* (New York: Crown, 1979), 171. I wish to thank Earle Labor, Wilson Professor of American Literature, Centenary College, and Sara S. Hodson, Curator of Literary Manuscripts, Huntington Library, for drawing my attention to some of the London/Burbank material mentioned here. I also thank the Huntington for permission to quote from Burbank's letter to London.

28. Ken Kraft and Pat Kraft, *Luther Burbank: The Wizard and the Man* (New York: Meredith Press, 1967), 116, 145.

29. Burbank, *The Training of the Human Plant* (New York: Century, 1907), 5. He also describes this new American hybridization process as "this marvelous mingling of races in the United States" (33).

30. London, *Bâtard and Other Stories* (Oakland: Star Rover House, 1987), 241. "Jees Uck," originally published in the magazine *The Smart Set* in September 1902, was included in London's third short story collection, *The Faith of Men and Other Stories* (1904). The character of Jees Uck represents an exception, of course, to London's tendency to create superior non-white protagonists only in stories set in warm climates.

31. "Koolau the Leper," in *The House of Pride*, 48. This story was initially published in the *Pacific Monthly* in December 1909.

32. McClintock, *White Logic: Jack London's Short Stories* (Grand Rapids, Mich.: Wolf House Books, 1975), 138.

33. Jack London, "Burns–Johnson Fight," in James Bankes, ed., *Jack London: Stories of Boxing* (Dubuque: William C. Brown, 1992), 145. All citations of London's boxing articles refer to this collection, unless otherwise noted.

34. This is not to say that London never lapses into stereotypes in this article: "[Johnson's] face beamed with all the happy, care-free innocence of a little child" (149). Given that London's career coincided with the height of the Jim Crow era, it is remarkable that his prose often escapes from racist language.

35. Phrases like "made noise with his fist like a lullaby" may seem clichéd, but remember that London was among those who invented such idioms.

36. "One criticism, and only one, can be passed upon Johnson. In the thirteenth round . . . [he] should have put Burns out. He could have put him out; it would have been child's play. Instead of which he let Burns live until the gong sounded, and in the opening of the fourteenth round the police stopped the fight and Johnson lost the credit of the knock-out" (150).

37. *Medford Sun* quoted in Bankes, *Stories of Boxing*, xii.

38. In his article on the fight itself (July 4), London heightens this contrast, noting that "the ferocity of the hairy-chested caveman and grizzly giant combined did not intimidate the cool-headed negro" (181).

39. Everhard, the self-educated protagonist of London's socialist novel, *The Iron Heel*, is a blacksmith and a brilliant strategist and theorist of revolution.

40. London, "The Mexican," in *The Night-Born*, 274. This story was first published in *The Saturday Evening Post*, August 19, 1911.

41. Harnish is the hero of London's *Burning Daylight* (1910). Stephen Knight, a mixed breed from the story "Aloha Oe," has a powerful physique of the more outwardly resplendent kind, and thus he is perhaps even more like London's Anglo-Saxon heroes.

42. I wish to thank the late Russ Kingman, of the Jack London Research Center, and I. Milo Shepard, London's literary executor, for allowing me to use the unpublished typescript of *Cherry*, from which all page numbers are taken. As of October 12, 1916, London had announced to Edgar G. Sisson, managing editor of *Collier's*, that he had completed 5,000 words of a new Hawaiian novel, for which he had "only begun to collect possible titles . . . *Cherry*; *The Screen-Lady*; *The Screen-Gazer*; and *Fire Dew*" (*Letters*, 3: 1588). A little more than a month before his death on November 22, 1916, he announced to Sisson that he had completed 15,000 words and was "swinging along on *Cherry*" (London to Sisson, October 23, 1916, *Letters*, 3: 1594).

43. London to the Members of the Local Glen Ellen Socialist Labor party, Mar. 17, 1916, *Letters*, 3: 1538.

CHRISTOPHER GAIR

The Wires Were Down: The Telegraph and the Cultural Self in "To Build a Fire" and White Fang

In every age since written language began, rhetorical forms have been to
a considerable extent influenced by the writing materials and the imple-
ments which were available for man's use. This is a familiar observation
in studies of the past. Is it not, then, time that somebody inquired into
the effects upon the form and substance of our present-day language of
the veritable maze of devices which have come into widely extended use
in recent years, such as the typewriter, with its invitation to the dictation
practice; shorthand, and, most important of all, the telegraph? Certainly
these agencies of expression cannot be without their marked and significant influences upon English style.
—Robert Lincoln O'Brien: "Machinery and English Style" (1904)[1]

There is a scene in Henry James' well known tale, "In The Cage" (1898),
when James' "obscure little public servant," the young telegraphist, whose
duty it is to "count words as numberless as the sands of the sea," speculates
on the "class that wired everything." Many of her wealthy customers spend
"pounds and pounds" on conveying "their expensive feelings" via telegraph,
in a story that clearly displays the rigid hierarchies of the English class
system. Fuelled by her reading of the romantic fiction she obtains from the
public library, the telegraphist reconstructs whole lives from the messages

From *Complicity and Resistance in Jack London's Novels: From Naturalism to Nature*, pp. 87–106.
Published by the Edwin Mellen Press. Copyright © 1997 by Christopher Gair.

73

she transmits, imaginatively filling in the spaces between the telegraphed words she sends.[2]

Though her readings prove illusory, for the obvious reason that the romantic novels she reads bear no relation to the actual lives of the upper classes, James' young woman's reconstructions neatly illustrate an essential function of another operative connected with telegraph technology. The invention of the telegraph in 1844, and more particularly its widespread use from around 1900,[3] created a new role for the journalist, and, to a large extent, brought about a reshaping of everyday perception and of use of language. Ultimately, the effects of telegraph technology permeated much of American culture, and helped to standardize ways of seeing the world. For in one respect, James' wealthy patrons of the Mayfair post office are atypical in their profligate approach to sending words down the wire. In general, the telegraph encouraged frugality with language, and, in its particular role as the conveyor of news, it necessitated the production of a discourse that could be understood and reproduced from coast to coast. Thus, James Carey has pointed out:

> The wire services demanded a form of language stripped of the local, the regional and colloquial. They demanded something closer to a "scientific" language, a language of strict denotation where the connotative features of utterance were under rigid control. . . . The telegraph, therefore, led to the disappearance of forms of speech and styles of journalism and story telling—the tall story, the hoax, much humor, irony and satire—that depended on a more traditional use of the symbolic. . . . The origins of objectivity may be sought . . . in the necessity of stretching language in space over the long lines of the Western Union.[4]

Because of the cost of sending messages, the correspondent who attended an event and provided detailed descriptions of it, was replaced by the "stringer," an expert in the supply of bare facts which could be embellished by newspapers of all denominations. At the far end of the line, the story would be reconstructed by a reporter using a concise prose developed in order to deal with the welter of news made available by the telegraph, in a process in which, as Carey points out, the "story [is] divorced from the storyteller."[5]

In this chapter, I shall suggest that the transformations associated with the telegraph not only re-structured the language of journalism, but also had a profound effect on the literary style of the early twentieth century. To illustrate the point, I want to focus, first, on the second, better known version of Jack London's short story, "To Build a Fire" (1908), in order to show how telegraph technology helped to shape both format and thematic features of

London's text. The sparseness of London's prose, the repetition of standard-ized phrases, the portrayal of the mechanisms of the mind and body, the use of communications metaphors, and the conclusion's separation of the pro-tagonist's mind and body can all be seen as manifestations of an ideology indelibly affected by the telegraph. In the second half of the chapter, I shall move on to a reading of *White Fang* (1906), both to develop and to qualify my assessment of the relationship between technology and London's fiction.

At first glance, it may appear that "To Build a Fire" is a curious choice of text, in a piece devoted to the impact of communications technology. Unlike "In the Cage," a tale that revolves around wires and communication, London's story is essentially a monologue. Told in the third person, it recounts the solo journey of an un-named man on an "exceedingly cold and gray" Arctic day.[6] The man has failed to heed the advice of an old-timer, who told him never to travel alone in the Klondike after fifty below. After condescendingly dismiss-ing the old-timer as being "rather womanish," and announcing to himself that "all a man had to do was keep his head, and he was all right" (470), the protagonist falls into a concealed spring. He knows that he must build a fire to thaw out, but his efforts fail, he runs in a panic to try to warm himself, but finally collapses through exhaustion. He admits that the old-timer was right—a companion could have built a fire and saved him—but the recogni-tion is too late and he freezes to death. "To Build a Fire" can thus be read as an example of the cautionary tale and, as such, catalogued neatly within a transhistorical sub-genre ranging back to Greek mythology, the Bible, and to ancient China, among many other examples.

A closer look at London's language, and at the forms of representation he reproduces, however, suggests that his text can be periodized as an example of an emergent literary discourse shaped by, but wary of, the new technol-ogy of the later nineteenth century. The prose is specific in its attention to "objective" detail, in a standardized language that constantly juxtaposes the quantifiable with the instinctual. The narrator tells us that the man is "with-out imagination" (463)—that is, he can absorb information without relating it to his own experience—before himself recording that it "was seventy-five below zero. Since the freezing point is thirty-two above zero, it meant that one hundred and seven degrees of frost obtained" (464). Throughout the text, the narrator repeatedly provides facts numerically—temperatures, times, dis-tances—in a narrative that seeks to persuade through weight of numbers, in the "scientific" language identified by Carey.

More pertinent still are the metaphors of communication with which London describes the man's body and other natural objects. In the soaking that leads to his death, the man wets his legs halfway to his knees, and tries to build a fire to dry himself. In the process, he feels his cheeks, nose and

fingers freezing, and is scarcely able to grip the twigs for the fire. In order
to ascertain whether he is holding the wood, the man has to "look and see."
The narrator comments, in a metaphor directly borrowed from the telegraph,
that the "wires were pretty well down between [the man] and his finger-ends"
(470), and communications between mind and body can only be maintained
through line-of-sight, in a retreat to bodily imitation of pre-electric, optical
telegraphs.[7]

Likewise, the series of events that culminates in the fire being extin-
guished is represented in the language of an imperceptible communications
system. In his hurry to warm himself, the man builds his fire under a spruce
tree, instead of in the open. The narrator describes how:

> the tree under which he had done this carried a weight of snow
> on its boughs. No wind had blown for weeks, and each bough was
> fully freighted. Each time he had pulled a twig he had communi-
> cated a slight agitation to the tree—an imperceptible agitation, so
> far as he was concerned, but an agitation sufficient to bring about
> the disaster. High up in the tree one bough capsized its load of
> snow. This fell on the boughs beneath, capsizing them. This process
> continued, spreading out and involving the whole tree. It grew like
> an avalanche, and it descended without warning upon the man and
> the fire, and the fire was blotted out! Where it had burned was a
> mantle of fresh and disordered snow. (471)

Like the telegraph, the tree is represented as communicating imperceptible
signs, which convey a message to another location, in this case, a bough high
in the spruce. It is only when this communication has been effected that the
avalanche descends on man and fire. The result, apart from the scattered
twigs, is that the man is "shocked" (471), an electrical impulse running
through the human body.

The analogy continues as the protagonist struggles to construct a second
fire. Once more, the narrator records that the man uses the "sense of vision in
place of that of touch," but on this occasion, his desire to close his fingers cannot be communicated to them, because "the wires were down, and the fingers
did not obey" (472). Representing the body as a system of communications
dependent on a network of wires, London equates the failure of that body
with a breakdown between centre and margin in cultural communications
networks. The man feels that it is "curious that one should have to use his
eyes in order to find out where his hands were" (475), because he has come to
rely on communications technology to provide information, and represents
his body as a similar model. Throughout the story, the protagonist—who is,

as we know, "without imagination"—has understood the volume of statistics merely as statistics, and it "never entered his head" (463) that they could be anything more than that. Without the data provided by the body as system now that the communications links have been broken, the man does what he warned himself against, he runs "blindly, without intention, in fear such as he had never known in his life" (475).

Even here, in his moment of panic, the protagonist is represented in metaphors frequently employed to describe electrical technology. In an echo of the Reverend Ezra S. Gannett's mid-nineteenth century sermon to his Boston congregation on electricity, "the swift winged messenger of destruction,"[8] the man seems "to himself to skim above the surface, and to have no connection with the earth," and compares himself with Mercury, the winged messenger "skimming over the earth." However, the flight cannot continue because, even if the man is unable to feel his body, he needs it to take him to safety. Without the ability to send messages to his extremities, the frozen parts extend, and he knows he will soon be "stiff and dead" (476).

It may already be apparent that there is a curiously double logic to the narrative of "To Build a Fire." On the one hand, the narrator uses the objective statistics of temperature, distance, and time to convey to the reader, in technical language, the difficulties facing the man. On the other, it is precisely this language, how it is communicated, and how it atrophies the imagination, that places the man in danger, and prevents him from acting. Shortly, I will demonstrate how London seeks to resolve this contradiction through a nostalgic call to pre-electric forms of communication, but first I will briefly outline the resolution to the story.

I

When the man realizes that he will die, he entertains the "conception of meeting death with dignity." He thinks that he has "been making a fool of himself, running around like a chicken with its head cut off," as he imagines it, and decides to "sleep off to death." The headless chicken simile initially seems strange, given that the narrator represents events through technological metaphors, and, anyway, it is the man's body that he has lost, rather than his head. However, the separation of head and body does suggest the limited degree to which the man experiences the running which his legs have undertaken, reminding us that he feels himself "skimming over the earth," and the reference to the reflexes of a decapitated chicken neatly links electrical impulses and bodily activity. In any case, the manner of his death quickly returns us to the telegraph and its effects. In what becomes an absolute separation of experience and perception, the man actually imagines himself with his colleagues as they discover his body:

He pictured the boys finding the body next day. Suddenly, he found himself with them, coming along the trail and looking for himself. And, still with them, he came around a turn in the trail and found himself lying in the snow. He did not belong with himself any more, for even then he was out of himself, standing with the boys and looking at himself in the snow. It certainly was cold, was his thought. When he got back to the States he could tell the folks what real cold was. He drifted on from this to a vision of the old-timer on Sulphur Creek. He could see him quite clearly, warm and comfortable and smoking a pipe.

"You were right, old hoss; you were right," the man mumbled to the old-timer of Sulphur Creek. (477)

As Lee Clark Mitchell points out, this passage represents a "disjuncture between spectator and actor,"[9] since the man's consciousness appears—at least imaginatively—to leave his body. With the inability to feel his body, the man becomes unable to resolve his dual status. By leaving his material self, that is "having no connection with the earth," he is able to telegraph himself through space (he is "suddenly" with his comrades), without actually having to—or even being able to—move his physical form.

On one level, this separation of participant and observer in naturalist fiction has been well documented. The naturalists' claims to scientific detachment have repeatedly been criticized, since, whilst demonstrating the horrors of the world, they simultaneously claim to be unable to correct injustice. However, in "To Build a Fire," it is necessary to move beyond Mitchell's formal duality and understand that the man's ability to recognize his position without being able to save himself is again an effect of new technology. In *The Incorporation of America* (1982), Alan Trachtenberg has argued that:

In technologies of communication, vicarious experience began to erode direct physical experience of the world. Viewing and looking at representations, words and images, city people found themselves addressed more and more often as passive spectators than as active participants, consumers of images and sensations produced by others. . . . The dailies dramatized a paradox of metropolitan life itself: the more knowable the world came to seem as *information*, the more remote and opaque it came to seem as *experience*.[10]

Thus, characters like Dreiser's George Hurstwood in *Sister Carrie* (1900) come to live their lives through the information they read in the newspapers, unable to experience the world at first hand. The process is self-perpetuating since Hurstwood's decline is equated with the diminishment of his space from a Chicago mansion to a flophouse bed, and is charted in the way that the newspaper becomes his sole contact with the outside world. As Philip Fisher has pointed out, for example, "[Hurstwood], so cut off from the world that he would rather not look out the window, reads in the newspapers that a bad storm is due, then in later editions that it has begun, then that it is a record storm, then that it will end soon, and finally that it has ended."[11]

As a *chechaquo*, or newcomer in the Northlands, the man in "To Build a Fire" is familiar with the statistics of the land, but not with its actualities. Thus, as we have seen, "Fifty degrees below zero was to him just precisely fifty degrees below zero" (463). Lacking in imagination, he is only able to register the numerical representation of cold, without being able to protect himself from that cold, or understand that he should not travel alone. The manner in which he spectates at his own death, and at the discovery of his own corpse reconfirms his position within a communications network separating experience and spectatorship. The protagonist can only experience his death at second hand, "looking at himself in the snow," and then report "what real cold was" (477) to the folks back home, in what develops into a procession of new representations of "cold" and death. Actual experience of either is denied. As with the paradox dramatized by the daily newspapers referred to by Trachtenberg, the man is able to know and understand his imminent demise as information, whilst simultaneously being unable to participate in it as experience.

As I have already intimated, however, there is another force at work in London's story. So far, I have focused on the ways in which telegraph technology—and also related developments such as the emergence of a new form of popular press—shape both language and experience in "To Build a Fire." To conclude my reading, I want to pay attention to the other impulse in the text, one that looks to instinct and companionship as alternatives to the isolated world of the reader of signs. Thus, I will examine both the way in which a dependence on signs contributes to the man's downfall, and the nostalgia for a world of face-to-face communication made increasingly difficult by the presence of vast communications networks.

II

It is the great irony of the text that in what Warren Susman calls "an age of easy and mass communications . . . when it appears that everyone can know what everyone else knows and everyone can know what everyone else thinks . . . no real, private, human communication is possible." The suggestion, as Susman makes clear in his work on the 1930s, is that "one makes the other impossible."[12] Thus, as we have seen, the man undertakes his fateful journey because he will not or can not listen to the advice of the old-timer. He chooses instead to rely on his own "judgement" (464), informed by the mass of statistics made available by contemporary technology. Rather than basing his actions on the knowledge gained through experience and imparted to the *chechaquo* on a one-to-one basis—that is, the traditional model of master and apprentice—the man makes his journey in full possession of all the facts (temperature, distance, time), but not of their implications. Because of the absence of first-hand experience in a world of mass communications, he does not recognize the worth of that experience until it is too late.

Likewise, his fall into the snow-covered spring can be read as an effect of a dependence on signs above instinct. Because of his faith in the quantifiable over the instinctual, the man is ill-equipped for the sign-less danger of the concealed spring. Although, early in the story, he does act instinctively, and shies "abruptly, like a startled horse" (466), because he feels the ice give under his feet, when he does fall through, it is at "a place where there were no signs, where the soft, unbroken snow seemed to advertise solidity beneath the man" (468–69). He is unable to anticipate the danger—cursing it as bad "luck" (469)—because he has internalized quantifiable sign-systems as the *only* way to read the world. His companion on the trip, a "big native husky," survives, it is suggested, because its (non-quantifiable) "instinct told it a truer tale than was told to the man by the man's judgement" (464), in a narrative which, despite its own use of the metaphors of mass communication, simultaneously manifests anxiety about the effects of that system. At the close of the story, the dog abandons the man's corpse and trots off to the camp, actually experiencing the journey as a participant in events. In contrast, the man can only project himself to his comrades, and act as a spectator at his own discovery, able to consume the images he projects, but unable to participate in his own body's experience.

The man's concluding thoughts do, however, suggest a recognition of the values threatened by mass communications technology. Although his reunion with "the boys" and his admission to the old-timer that his advice was right (477) are only simulacra of actual meetings, made possible by telegraphing the mind in an imaginary break between communication and transportation—that is, the separation made possible by the telegraph—they also demonstrate a yearning for the personal and private relationships threatened by that technology. Thus while recent readings of "To Build a Fire" as taking what Mark Seltzer has called the "mathematical form of a count-down or calibrated dissipation of energy within a closed system. . . . as the system—[that is] the natural body . . .—approaches degree-zero or entropy,"[13] are in one way correct, they fail to register the text's attempts to escape this form. By implying that the man could have survived if he had been able to participate within older forms of communication, and by imparting this recognition into his dying consciousness, London's text both demonstrates the degree of penetration of ways of thought promoted by the telegraph and other new technologies, and the dangers associated with such forms of consciousness. To use London's own metaphor in a slightly different manner from that he employs in the story, for the protagonist of "To Build a Fire," imaginatively conversing with colleagues and old-timer alike, and no longer reliant on the information provided by mass communications systems, the wires are down.

III

If we were to see the narrative voice in "To Build a Fire" as a "personality," then clearly that personality is one defined by his contradictions. Like Walter Benjamin's "angel of history," on the one hand he displays a yearning for the past while on the other, a "storm irresistibly propels him into the future to which his back is turned, while the pile of debris before him grows skyward. This storm is what we call progress."[14] Thus, as with the narrators examined by Susan L. Mizruchi in *The Power of Historical Knowledge* (1988), London's storyteller points "both into and out of [his] ideological bind."[15] Seeking to evade the historical entrapment of the protagonist, the narrator can only do so by engaging in his own evasions, at once denying and employing a consciousness produced by a particular cultural and technological structure. Like Mizruchi's chosen novelists (Hawthorne, James, and Dreiser), there is a constant ambivalence within London's work, which I have defined according to the contradictory demands of production and consumption economies.

In order to develop my reading of this contradictory consciousness, I now wish to turn to *White Fang*, a novel that both highlights and re-situates the claims of social ties, and that is both contained by its period of production, and seeks alternatives to the effects of this containment. About halfway through the book, the eponymous wolf-dog falls into the possession of "Beauty" Smith, a violent "monstrosity" of a man, "known far and wide as the weakest of weak-kneed and snivelling cowards."[16] Smith confines the animal in a cage and forces him to fight to the death with "all sizes and breeds of dogs." Bar his final contest, when he is rescued from the massive jaws of a bull-dog by the intervention of the mining engineer, Weedon Scott, White Fang kills all his opponents. Of course, on one level, the scene is a perfect demonstration of naturalist Darwinian theory in practice. White Fang survives because of his ferocity and because of "his capacity for being moulded by the pressure of environment" (219). His greatest advantage is "experience" (220), which enables him to anticipate any of the tricks of the other dogs. Concerned with "how" rather than "why" things happen (137), White Fang unsurprisingly resembles the dog in "To Build a Fire" in his capacity for survival.

However, the novel can be read in a somewhat different manner, in order to question the equation of instinct and experience with survival as witnessed in "To Build a Fire". As in James' tale, the cage in which White Fang is trapped is far more than a material construction of metal bars. Like James' young woman, the wolf-dog is depersonalized by the men outside the cage, who employ him in a purely functional role, in this case as entertainer and focus of gambling. In this sense, the cage can be regarded as a synecdochal part of a cultural whole limiting individual action and fostering a network of ideological entrapment. For White Fang to prosper, it is necessary for him to break free not only from the cage, but also from the metaphorical prison constructed out of his experience of the world. To liberate himself from the position of object of speculation, White Fang must unlearn that combination of instinct and experience that were the enabling conditions for survival in "To Build a Fire," and that here turn the wolf-dog into a fighting brute. Thus, he must unlearn the very lessons of Social Darwinism that seem essential in "To Build a Fire," in *The Call of the Wild*, and in the early chapters of *White Fang*, if he is to escape from being forever the brutalized Other. In order to do so, he must be represented in a rather different relationship with technology from that of either dog or man in "To Build a Fire."

The most obvious clue to this difference resides in the contrasting nature and fate of the central human protagonists. In "To Build a Fire," as we have seen, the man is a nameless newcomer to the Northlands, who relies on statistics to guide him through an alien landscape. His knowledge is no compensation for the lack of experience of the Arctic winter and he dies as a direct result of his misguided faith in figures. In *White Fang*, the man is also a newcomer, named Weedon Scott; he is a mining engineer, bringing the latest technological advances to his work, able to succeed in a hostile environment with which he is unfamiliar because his knowledge can tame that environment. Whereas the technological metaphors employed in "To Build a Fire" represent the body as a communications network unable to cope with the demands of the Klondike, Scott's bodily machinery perfectly equips him for battles with land and people alike. Thus, when he rescues White Fang from Smith and the bull-dog, Scott's power is depicted in the image of the man-machine:

> He was in a rage himself—a sane rage. His gray eyes seemed metallic and steel-like as they flashed upon the crowd. . . .
> The crowd began to grow unruly, and some of the men were protesting against the spoiling of the sport; but they were silenced when the newcomer lifted his head from his work for a moment and glared at them. (227)

Scott prospers in the Klondike because of his internalization of the statistics of disciplinary individualism, which transform him into master of man and nature alike. In *White Fang*, there is no tension in the relationship between narrative thrust and modern systems of production. Scott is unproblematically a reflex of his machine culture, able to bring the efficiency of time and motion into his job and his body. The Veblenesque "instinct of workmanship" identifiable in *The Call of the Wild* and in the early chapters of *White Fang* has been transformed into the culturalism of the scientific management of a highly disciplined self.

One side-effect of this shift is to make *White Fang* an endorsement of an already established social order. Scott's power depends not only on his own actions, but also on the system to which they belong. When he saves White Fang from Smith, he is virtually unchallenged because of his place in the existing hierarchy:

> Some of the men were already departing; others stood in groups, looking on and talking. Tim Keenan joined one of the groups.
> "Who's that mug?" he asked.
> "Weedon Scott," some one answered.
> "And who in the hell is Weedon Scott?" the faro-dealer demanded.
> "Oh, one of them crack-a-jack minin' experts. He's in with all the big bugs. If you want to keep out of trouble, you'll steer clear of him, that's my talk. He's all hunky with the officials. The Gold Commissioner's a special pal of his."
> "I thought he must be somebody," was the faro-dealer's comment. "That's why I kept my hands offen him at the start" (230–31).

Later in the novel, when Scott returns to California, his social status—already implied by his command of standard(ized) English—is confirmed. His father is a judge, and the family lives on a large estate. The ability to convert disciplinary individualism into large personal profit is revealed as a class privilege, permitting the expensive training of the skilled specialist. Whereas Mark Seltzer sees in naturalism, the "anti-biological and technological making of men and the replacement of the mother by the machine,"[17] Scott epitomizes the fusion of the two. It is only because he has a mother and, more importantly, father who belong to a particular social group, that Scott is made into the type of technological man he becomes.

In the early chapters of the novel, White Fang's development is portrayed in a different manner. He is shaped according to by now familiar responses to internal and external forces. Thus, the young cub acts according to his desires (for food, play, etc.), and fears (such as the cuff of his mother's paw when he strays too near the entrance to the cave). He will only perform a function because he wants to, or because he is compelled to do so. The "restrictions of life" are "laws," such as those Buck learns in *The Call of the Wild*. Even before he leaves the cave where he was born, White Fang commences the process of "classification" based on instinct and experience:

> Hunger he had known; and when he could not appease his hunger he had felt restriction. The hard obstruction of the cave-wall, the sharp nudge of his mother's nose, the smashing stroke of her paw, the hunger unappeased of several famines, had borne in upon him that all was not freedom in the world, that to life there were limitations and restraints. These limitations and restraints were laws. To be obedient to them was to escape hurt and make for happiness.

In each instance, behaviour is represented in terms of a "natural" response to external forces, manifested in an "instinct" passed "down to him from a remote ancestry through a thousand thousand lives" (139). Survival depends on acting "naturally," and on avoiding encounters with creatures more powerful than himself.

From the moment that he is rescued, however, White Fang begins to adopt the culturalism of his new master, and to reject actions based on instinct and past experience. Instead of the "natural" responses to instinctive desires that shape the "voracious appetite" of life in the wild (153), White Fang must learn, as Seltzer points out, to "love pain and the god-like hand of his master." Thus:

> White Fang learns to love at once the pleasure of unnatural acts (acts contrary to every "mandate of his instinct") and the pain of turning from "the natural" to "the cultural."[18]

He moves from absolute certainty about the accuracy of his instinct, through being "torn by conflicting feelings, impulses" when Scott pats him (an act "distasteful to his instinct"), until, finally, the wolf-dog undergoes a "revolution" in which he has "to ignore the urges and promptings of instinct and reason, defy experience, give the lie to life itself" (240–42). In this final state, White Fang will even forego meat to be with "his god" (244). In accepting and internalizing the disciplinary individualism of his master, the wolf-dog abandons the will to self-preservation manifested by Buck and the dog in "To Build a Fire," and adopts the responses necessary for existence in "civilized" California, where the concluding chapters of the novel take place. To be a "cultural" being is to be an "unnatural" one.

The move to California is depicted in the terms of the immigrant's arrival in an America fraught with technological dangers. Initially deciding to leave White Fang in the Northlands, Scott fears the results of taking a "wolf" home. Musing on the punishments for transgression in a country where law and the discipline of Systematic Management go hand in hand, he fears White Fang killing other dogs—an action that would result in legal action against Scott, and electrocution for his pet (250). On arrival in San Francisco, White Fang is "appalled" and "bewildered" by the "towering buildings" and the "thunder of the streets" (255). Repeating the fears of "unnatural" urban existence familiar both from the sociological writings of Georg Simmel, and from the contemporaneous fiction of Theodore Dreiser and Upton Sinclair, London represents White Fang's experiences in terms of confusion and powerlessness.

In an echo of the "Melting Pot" ideology of acculturation, however, White Fang is soon able to throw off the final shackles of instinct and adopt the rationalized persona of the disciplined individual, even able to resist the temptations of the chicken-yard (266–67). Again, this transformation is represented in terms of the discipline necessary to become a cultural being:

> Life was complex in the Santa Clara Valley after the simplicities of the Northland. And the chief thing demanded by these intricacies of civilization was control, restraint—a poise of self that was as delicate as the fluttering of gossamer wings and at the same time as rigid as steel. . . . Life flowed past him, deep and wide and varied, continually impinging upon his senses, demanding of him instant and endless adjustments and correspondences, and compelling him, almost always, to suppress his natural impulses. (268)

Whereas for the man in "To Build a Fire," the suppression of instinct is life-threatening, for White Fang it is the ticket to prosperity and contentment in California. Far from being the loner of the Klondike, who shuns all contact, he becomes, at the end of the novel, the "well-adjusted" communal being, licking his puppy's face (284).[19]

IV

It should already be apparent that the transformation of White Fang, and the deployment of statistical and disciplinary individualism in the novel embrace the technological and quantifiable world in a way antithetical to the doubtful narrative voice of "To Build a Fire." Where that voice was split between caution at, and employment of the new language of communications systems, the narrator of *White Fang* unequivocally endorses the standardization and control of individual actions (even implying that such behaviour is the enabling condition for companionship rather than its antithesis). It is therefore unsurprising that James Carey's account of the impact of the wire service on the use of language should closely resemble the impact of technology on lifestyle. To recap, Carey wrote of a "form of language stripped of the local, the regional and colloquial," able to be understood from coast to coast. Likewise, the Systematic Management used to produce specialists like Weedon Scott both demands such a language and produces standardized "individuals," each able to understand and act upon instructions in a regimented, interchangeable manner. From this perspective, *White Fang* may be regarded as an endorsement of such standardization unmatched by London's other works. To close this chapter, however, I want to develop a somewhat different feature of the novel, one that moves away from and compensates for the monotony of this standardization of language and daily life. Throughout my readings of London's early, "naturalist" texts—that is, throughout Section Two of this study—I have been concerned with the shared logic of consumer capitalism and linguistic reproduction. Discussing both *The Call of the Wild* and *The Sea-Wolf,* I pointed out the determined meaning of narrative closure, highlighting the repetition of various generic prerequisites. The ending to *White Fang,* repackaging the domestic bliss implied by the conclusions to "South of the Slot" and *The Sea-Wolf,* is once more an "inevitable" ending to a standardized structural construction. As with Humphrey Van Weyden, White Fang must be contained within a particular role-figure if he is to meet the standards of "civilization." There is a fusion of formal and thematic order within a cultural whole demanding consistency and predictability.

Daniel J. Boorstin has identified various activities through which Americans "hoped to find a residual stock of the unrepeatable and the unpredictable." Charting the popularization of sports, the sensationalizing of reporting of crime, and the obsession with weather-forecasting as forms of compensation for "lives of increasingly repeatable packaged experience,"[20] Boorstin sees such interests as meeting fundamental human needs. While such essentializing is certainly questionable, and we may prefer to regard the desire for sensationalist accounts (themselves packaged within an endlessly repeatable format) as residual traces of experiences denied under increasingly reified daily life, Boorstin's account tarries with a steady stream of allusions to "chance" in *White Fang.* For example, we have already seen that White Fang is placed in a cage in order to satisfy the prospectors' craving for gambling, an activity bringing unpredictability to an otherwise seemingly unvarying white landscape. Likewise, the fight with the bull-dog only ends as it does because of the fortuitous arrival of Scott and his companion when White Fang appears defeated (226–30).

Indeed, despite the learning process undertaken by the wolf-dog, a process depending first on "the act of classification" (137), and later upon mistrusting "instinct," survival is ultimately determined by the fact that "with live things events were somehow always happening differently" (129). These contradictory desires—to make experience endlessly repeatable (and thus predictable and manageable), and to randomize it—are best illustrated in a short passage depicting the reunion of White Fang and his first human master, the Indian, Gray Beaver:

> Gray Beaver had intended camping that night on the far bank of the Mackenzie, for it was in that direction that the hunting lay. But on the near bank, shortly before dark, a moose, coming down to drink, had been espied by Kloo-kooch, who was Gray Beaver's squaw. Now, had not the moose come down to drink, had not Mit-sah been steering out of the course because of the snow, had not Kloo-kooch sighted the moose, and had not Gray Beaver killed it with a lucky shot from his rifle, all subsequent things would have happened differently. Gray Beaver would not have camped on the near side of the Mackenzie, and White Fang would have passed by and gone on, either to die, or to find his way to his wild brothers and become one of them,—a wolf to the end of his days. (181)

Although this passage reduces each random event to an item in a catalogue of chance happenings ("had not . . . had not . . . had not . . ." etc.), it does so in a manner that insists on the separation of action from the merely quantifiable and classifiable. It represents a scene where intentions and effects come together, but it does so in a way that qualifies the causal relationship between the two. White Fang desires companionship, but runs "blindly. . . . blundering in the darkness" (180) in the hope of satisfaction. It is only the conflation of a series of unpredictable events that permits the eventual "freedom" of choice allowed to him in preferring the "civilized" to the "wild." Paradoxically, the arbitrariness that helps to make actions free, as Walter Benn Michaels has pointed out with reference to *The House of Mirth*, also "threaten[s] to make them random and thus . . . not really actions at all."[21] Nevertheless, chance does offer an escape from the welter of statistics used to quantify and order the world elsewhere in London's writing, and in the culture of which it was a part. It is the element of chance—whether White Fang will find Gray Beaver; whether he will live or die; whether he will be dog or wolf—that makes the result of his journey unpredictable and "exciting," both for him and for the reader.

Finally, it is this link (between actor and spectator) and its limits that differentiates White Fang from the protagonists of "To Build a Fire." Whereas the man in the story becomes "pure" spectator, witnessing his own death and discovery, and the dog is represented as "pure" participant, free from the sign-system that condemns its master, White Fang fuses the roles of performer (the "character" acting out intentions) and spectator (witnessing the results of what he has done). For in itself, neither half of this dual presence satisfactorily explains what happens. To adapt Michaels' reading of Crane's "Five White Mice," White Fang's reunion with Gray Beaver is "not exactly unintended"—in that case it would not be an act—but it is "weak in intentionality." Because he makes the decision to run in one direction, we can think of White Fang trying to find Gray Beaver, but to think of him as intending to do so implies a control that is absent, and to imagine him hoping to appears to eliminate his role altogether. Like gambling in Michaels' reading of Crane, the attraction of chance in White Fang is that it "cannot be reduced to either intending or hoping."[22]

It is this ambiguity that prevents the dismissal of the novel as being a straightforward endorsement of the logic of disciplinary individualism. The weak intentionality of White Fang's search may well share a cultural desire to participate in the speculative economy of statistical probability, but it also resists this impulse. On the one hand, White Fang's action mimics the function of the "professional gambler," that fusion of the expert calculator of odds and the passive spectator at say, the commodities market or the spinning of a wheel. On the other, it is an illustration of his own subjectivity, freed from the confines of Systematic Management. It thus at once establishes a link and a difference between naturalism and other forms of social practice, and claims a (limited) space for individual agency in an increasingly disciplined community. Although the naturalist narratives I have examined in this section share the logic of reproduction and reduction—the economy of the telegraph, the mass production of formula fictions and other commodities, etc.—they can also offer alternatives to these reifying processes.

Notes

1. Quoted in Mark Seltzer: *Bodies and Machines*, London: Routledge, 1992, pp. 6–7.

2. Henry James: "In the Cage", in James: *Selected Tales*, selected by Peter Messent and Tom Paulin, London: Dent, 1982, pp. 119–27, p. 119, p. 130.

3. See Douglass Tallack: *Twentieth Century America: The Intellectual and Cultural Context*, London: Longman, 1991, p. 29; Ian F.A. Bell: *Henry James and the Past: Readings into Time*, London: Macmillan, 1991, pp. 66–69.

4. James W. Carey: "Technology and Ideology: The Case of the Telegraph", in *Prospects*, Volume 8, 1983, pp. 303–25, p. 310.

5. Ibid., p. 311.

6. Jack London: "To Build a Fire", in London: *Novels and Stories*, edited by Donald Pizer, Cambridge: Library of America, 1982, pp. 462–78, p. 462. Subsequent page numbers are referred to in parentheses in the text. "To Build a Fire" first appeared in *Century Magazine*, 76 (August, 1908), pp. 525–34. The first book edition text, of which this is a reprint, was in *Lost Face*, New York: Macmillan, 1910.

7. Carey points out (p. 313) that: "Virtually any American city of any vintage has a telegraph hill or a beacon hill reminding us of such [line-of-sight] devices. They relied on shutters, flaps, disks, or arms operating as for semaphoric signalling at sea. They were optical rather than "writing at a distance" systems and the forerunners of microwave networks, which rely on relay stations on geographic high points for aerial transmissions." The first line-of-sight telegraph to come into practical use in America was established in 1800, between Martha's Vineyard and Boston. By 1812, there were plans for a telegraph linking Maine and New Orleans. In *The Sea-Wolf* (1904, also in *Novels and Stories*, pp. 479–771), London employs the same telegraph metaphors to chart the decline of Wolf Larsen. As Larsen's bodily systems shut down, one-by-one, until he is left with his "intelligence . . . disembodied" (764), dialogue and narrator record that, "the lines are going down, breaking bit by bit communication with the world" (753); "the wires were like the stock market, now up, now down. . . . we would wait for the connection to be reestablished" (756); "[His spirit] would flutter and live till the last line of communication was broken, and after that who was to say how much longer it might continue to flutter and live?" (760). This breakdown in communications is accompanied by a shift from acting to being:

> No more would he conjugate the verb "to do" in every mood and tense. "To be" was all that remained to him—to be, as he had defined death, without movement; to will, but not to execute, to think and reason and in the spirit of him to be as alive as ever, but in the flesh to be dead, quite dead (754).

As will become apparent through my reading of "To Build a Fire", this condition is also linked closely to the effects of telegraph technology.

8. Carey, p. 108.

9. Quoted in June Howard: *Form and History in American Literary Naturalism*, Chapel Hill: University of North Carolina Press, 1985, p. 197, n. 22. Mitchell develops this point—without specifically referring to this passage—in "Imposing (on) Events in London's 'To Build a Fire'", Chapter 2 of his *Determined Fictions: American Literary Naturalism*, New York: Columbia University Press, 1989, pp. 34–54.

10. Alan Trachtenberg: *The Incorporation of America: Culture and Society in the Gilded Age*, New York: Hill and Wang, 1982, p. 122, p. 125.

11. Philip Fisher: "Acting, Reading, Fortune's Wheel: *Sister Carrie* and the Life History of Objects", in Eric J. Sundquist (ed): *American Realism: New Essays*, Baltimore: Johns Hopkins University Press, 1982, pp. 259–77, pp. 274–75.

12. Warren Susman: *Culture as History: The Transformation of American Society in the Twentieth Century*, New York: Pantheon, 1984, p. 261.

13. Seltzer, pp. 224–25, n. 37. . . .

14. Walter Benjamin: "Theses on the Philosophy of History", in Benjamin: *Illuminations*, with an Introduction by Hannah Arendt, London: Fontana, 1992, pp. 245–55, p. 249.

15. Susan L. Mizruchi: *The Power of Historical Knowledge: Narrating the Past in Hawthorne, James, and Dreiser*, Princeton: Princeton University Press, 1988, p. 25.

16. Jack London: *White Fang*, in *Novels and Stories*, pp. 87–284, p. 209. Subsequent page numbers are provided in parentheses in the text. *White Fang* was serialized in *Outing Magazine*, between May and September, 1906. The first book edition, of which this is a reprint, was New York: Macmillan, 1906.

17. Seltzer, p. 188.

18. Ibid., p. 169.

19. June Howard points out (p. 57) that, "Collie's puppies by White Fang—five-eighths dog, three-eighths wolf—mediate between nature and culture not only by mingling the heredity of dog and wolf, but also by creating a family that mimics the values of human domesticity."

20. Daniel J. Boorstin: *The Americans: The Democratic Experience*, New York: Random House, 1973, p. 407, p. 402.

21. Walter Benn Michaels: *The Gold Standard and the Logic of Naturalism: American Literature at the Turn of the Century*, Berkeley: University of California Press, 1987, p. 232. Michaels continues: "To give up agency for freedom seems a paradoxically heavy price to pay; in what sense is an agent free if he isn't free to act?"

22. Ibid., pp. 236–37.

JAMES A. PAPA JR.

Canvas and Steam: Historical Conflict in Jack London's Sea-Wolf

Jack London's *Sea-Wolf* (1904) is one of America's best known sea tales. The novel, inspired in part by London's own experience on a sealer at the age of seventeen, is set aboard a sealing schooner called the *Ghost* in the Northern Pacific at the turn of the century. The novel's plot chronicles the transformation of a bookish shipwreck victim into a strong and able sailor at the hands of a cruel but intellectually brilliant skipper, Wolf Larsen.

Humphrey Van Weyden, or Hump—the castaway—is plucked from the foggy waters of San Francisco Bay by the outward-bound *Ghost* following the wreck of a cross-bay ferry, the *Martinez*, on which he was a passenger. Short one man because of the untimely death of a crewman who had the audacity, or perhaps the luck, to die at the very start of the ship's voyage, Larsen orders Hump pressed into service as a cabin boy, despite his protests, instead of ferrying him back to shore.

From this point on, the literate Van Weyden serves as a foil for Larsen, a self-taught philosopher taken by the current intellectual trends of his time, most notably the rise of Social Darwinism. Larsen shares with Melville's Ahab a perverted passion for the ideal, and each is finally rendered a "grotesque," to quote from Sherwood Anderson's "Book of the Grotesques," by their distorted pursuit of personal truths. In Larsen's case, this perversion

From *Midwest Quarterly* 40, no. 3 (1999): 274–84. Copyright © 1999 by *Midwest Quarterly*.

of thought is portrayed metaphorically by the brain tumor that ultimately destroys him. Until that time, the novel's plot revolves in good part around the struggle between Wolf Larsen and Hump over whose philosophy of life is correct. Paradoxically, the struggle manifests itself through repeated physical conflict in which Hump is forced to develop his own physical powers. As an added twist, engineered to satisfy popular readers, Hump and Wolf also compete for the affections of Maud Brewster, a woman survivor from the *Martinez* hauled aboard soon after Hump. In the end, Wolf dies of illness, the *Ghost* is wrecked, and Hump and Maud are rescued.

It is the contest between Wolf and his brother, Death, also the skipper of a sealer, which is the focus of this essay. The historical conflict between sail and steam, played out in the contest on the sealing grounds between Wolf's schooner and the steamship *Macedonia*, captained by Death, has until now been overlooked. However, when looked at closely this battle, which ends with the triumph of the *Macedonia*, can be said to both eclipse and undermine the novel's apparent primary concern with the ideological struggle between Van Weyden's idealism and Larsen's Social Darwinism, of which so many critics have made note. London himself, quoted from a letter to Mary Austin in Phillip S. Foner's *Jack London: American Rebel*, referred to *The Sea-Wolf* as an "[attack] on Nietzschean philosophy" (63). But a careful exploration of the contest between the *Ghost* and the *Macedonia* will illustrate how this seemingly minor thread in the narrative actually betrays the novel's deeper preoccupations.

The Sea-Wolf was published in 1904, when the era of sail was coming to a close in terms of commercial enterprise. In a very real sense it was already past. Though large numbers of vessels in the maritime continued to carry sail, the steamship had already laid irrevocable claim to the high seas, and the next decade or so would see large numbers of sailing vessels scuttled or converted to steam. The reasons for this are simple: steamships traveled faster, were more dependable, and required much smaller crews. In the sealing industry, where profits often approached forty per cent, the vessels of choice were schooners and sloops, boats easily "managed by one or two men" while the hunters were out on the sea (Busch, 137, 140; Chapelle, 220). Still, some sealers were converting to steam as early as the 1880s. Because the sealing industry as a whole, at least in the north Pacific, was effectively finished by the end of the nineteenth century, complete dominance by the steamship was never achieved, and most sealers remained sailing vessels.

The sailor Johnson, one of Wolf Larsen's crew, extols the virtues of the *Ghost* under sail. She is "considered the fastest schooner in both the San Francisco and Victoria fleets," and was "once a private yacht . . . built for speed" (London, 47). Given that the major sealing ports in North America at the time were San Francisco and Victoria, British Columbia, the claim carries weight. But the *Ghost* is still no match for the *Macedonia*, whose steam engines render her capable of "pounding through the sea at a seventeen-knot gait" (London, 189).

Pardoxically, though the *Macedonia* represents the new era of steam and mechanical propulsion on the high seas, we never get a clear sighting or a detailed description of her. In fact, the crew of the *Sea-Wolf* never sees anything of the *Macedonia* but "smoke" on the horizon (173). For the moment, the encroaching steam age, with its reliance on mechanical ability and rational thought, qualities at odds with both Wolf's Social Darwinism and the romance of sail, remains a distant, if inevitable, threat.

The irony is that the *Macedonia*, propelled by great engines and able to traverse the sea at will, should receive such ephemeral treatment in the novel, while the *Ghost*, a vessel driven by sail and dependent upon the vagaries of the wind, is described in concrete detail:

> The *Ghost* is an eight-ton schooner of a remarkably fine model. The beam, or width, is twenty-three feet, and her length a little over ninety feet. A lead keel of fabulous but unknown weight makes her very stable, while she carries an immense spread of canvas. From the deck to the top of the maintopmast is something over a hundred feet, while the foremast with its topmast is eight or ten feet shorter. (48)

Such a description contradicts the very essence of her name, which suggests she is no longer a material force in the world. In truth, the *Macedonia*, ever hidden beneath the horizon's rim but for the smoke from her stacks, is the more ghost-like of the two vessels.

But it is in this very contradiction between expectations and reality that the nature of the historical conflict is made clear. Wolf Larsen's era is about to be eclipsed by a new one that he knows nothing of, an era in which the world will be run by men like his brother, Death, who, except for his brutish nature, remains a mystery even to Wolf:

> "Death Larsen," [Hump] involuntarily cried. "Is he like you?"
> "Hardly. He is a lump of an animal without any head. He has all my—my—"
> "Brutishness," [Hump] suggested.
> "Yes—Thank you for the word—all my brutishness, but he can scarcely read or write."
> "And he has never philosophized on life," [Hump] added.

"No," Wolf Larsen answered with an incredible air of sadness. "And he is all the more happier for leaving life alone. He is too busy living life to think about it. My mistake was in ever opening up books." (84)

Death, in his mechanical steamship on the horizon, is the new twentieth-century man. He is more brutal in his rational mechanistic approach to life than Wolf, in his animalism, can ever be. There is no room, and no need, for philosophy or poetry in Death Larsen's world.

The transition from sail to steam at this same moment in history only serves to reinforce this assault on the intellect and the soul. Faster passages under steam mean less time at sea, and less time for reflection and the kind of deep thinking that lends itself not only to the philosophizing of Wolf Larsen, but also to the poetic gleanings of Melville's Ishmael atop a masthead of the *Pequod*. The traditional sea voyage, since the time of Ulysses "a natural vehicle for the human imagination exploring the unknown, whether it be discovering new continents [or] finding out the truth about oneself" (Carlson, 5), is about to be transformed into a purely technical endeavor, with no goal other than the quick and efficient transfer of cargo or passengers for one port to another.

Viewed in this manner, any reading of the novel as a romance suffers a strange twist. Whereas many critics see Hump as the romantic hero, a case can now be made for Wolf assuming that role *if* we focus on the historical moment under discussion here—the displacement of the nineteenth century and the age of sail by the twentieth century and the age of steam. In the new era, man will no longer look outside of himself to nature for spiritual salvation, as Wolf comes close to doing on the *Ghost* one "blazing tropic night":

> Do you know, I am filled with a strange uplift; I feel as if all time were running through me, as though all powers were mine. I know truth, divine good from evil, right from wrong. My vision is clear and far. I could almost believe in God. . . . (London, 62)

The potential ability of a long passage under sail to induce religious or mystical feelings in a man, even one as cruel as Wolf Larsen, simply by immersing him in the natural rhythms of life at sea, is about to be lost.

In their preoccupation with the novel as a clash between Wolf Larsen's materialism and the idealism of Humphrey Van Weyden, and with the transformation of Hump from a bookish kind of gentleman to a lion-like hero, critics have neglected the historical conflict between Wolf and his brother, Death. The contest between Wolf and Hump is only one conflict in the text, and the two, far from being opponents, are actually unknowning victims of the new era represented by the *Macedonia*'s smokestack on the horizon. The coming age is a threat both to Hump's moral idealism—it has no use for books and ideas—and to Wolf's glorification of physical strength, which Hump eventually comes to appreciate in his own way:

> Once more the *Ghost* bore away before the storm, this time so submerging herself that for some seconds I thought she would never reappear. Even the wheel, quite a deal higher than the waist, was covered and swept again and again. At such moments I felt strangely alone with God, alone with him and watching the chaos of his wrath. And then the wheel would reappear, and Wolf Larsen's broad shoulders, his hands gripping the spokes and holding the schooner to the course of his will, himself an earth god, dominating the storm, flinging its descending waters from him and riding it to his own ends. And oh, the marvel of it! The marvel of it! That tiny men should live and breathe and work, and drive so small a contrivance of wood and cloth through so tremendous an elemental strife. (135)

The old saying that wooden ships make iron men proves itself true here. The new ships will not need men with the strength nor the courage to climb the rigging, haul in the sheets, or wrestle with the wheel or tiller on deck in a blow. Instead, the sailor so heroically depicted in this passage will soon become nothing more than a slave to a machine, imprisoned below decks to stoke the burners and tend to the engines of the new ships. There will be no more men like Melville's Bulkington, who wrestles the ship's wheel in a blow to get her free of a lee shore. The age of Melville, London, Dana, and Slocum has come to a close.

That Hump is in league with Wolf in decrying what is to come is evident in his use of the word "enemy" to describe the *Macedonia* and her crew in his account of Wolf's attempt to shanghai some of his brother's men:

> Even the [*Ghost*'s] hunters were pulling, and with three pairs of oars in the water they rapidly overhauled what I may appropriately term the enemy. (181)

Hump has become, for better or worse, a member of the "little floating world" (48) that the *Ghost* represents, and his solidarity with it, against the larger threat of the new machine age, whose influence the sea has so far resisted, is clear.

If the new era has no time for the romantic musings of Humphrey Van Weyden, it also devalues physical strength. An individual's ability to physically enforce his will upon others, upon which Wolf's conception of Darwinism is based, no longer means anything. For Wolf, power resides primarily, if not solely, in a man's ability to impose his will on the world and on others through pure physical strength. We see this demonstrated over and over again in the novel. The first instance is in Wolf's early assault on the cabin boy, Leach, at Leach's refusal to take on duties he had not contracted for when he signed up for the voyage:

> Then came another stirring of Wolf Larsen's tremendous strength. It was utterly unexpected, and it was over and done with between the ticks of two seconds. He had sprung fully six feet across the deck and driven his fist into the other's stomach.... The cabin boy—and he weighed one hundred and sixty-five at the very least—crumpled up. His body wrapped limply about the fist like a wet rag about a stick. He lifted into the air, described a short curve, and struck the deck alongside the corpse ... where he lay and writhed about in agony. (28–29)

Thus, Leach falls in line, and accepts his newly acquired duties as a puller, leaving Hump to serve, however unwillingly, as the new cabin boy: "What was I to do? To be brutally beaten, to be killed perhaps, would not help my case" (30).

It might be argued that to subdue Hump forcefully is no special feat, that Wolf's physical power here is no real asset. But over and over again we see Larsen challenge the sailors physically and defeat them. He repeatedly battles Leach on deck, and at one point he manages to fight off a good portion of the crew single-handedly when he is jumped by them in the forecastle (109–11). Even at the end of the text, when Hump has become much stronger than the day he was fished cold, wet, and frightened out of the sea by Wolf, he still fears, and rightly so, Larsen's tremendous physical strength, despite the fact that the captain of the *Ghost* at that point is blind and near death.

But Wolf's strength serves him only on board the *Ghost*, whose decks represent an era which, if it is not fully past, is in its final moment. Against Death and his ship, Wolf does not even attempt to try his strength. Instead, he drives the *Ghost* into the fog banks, fleeing the bright "sunshine, the clear sky ..., the sea breaking and rolling wide to the horizon" in order to escape from the *Macedonia*, which "vomiting smoke and fire and iron missiles" is "rushing madly upon" his ship (189). Larsen knows the *Ghost* cannot hope to win against the mechanically powered ship, so he sails her into the mist in a desperate attempt to deny the reality bearing down upon him. The metaphorical implications of this maneuver are not lost on Hump:

> The mind recoiled from contemplation of a world beyond this wet veil which wrapped us around. This was the world, the universe itself, its bounds so near one felt impelled to reach out both arms and push them back. It was impossible that the rest could be beyond these walls of gray. The rest was a dream, no more than the memory of a dream. (189)

Earlier in the text the fog is described in similar terms during Hump's trip across the bay on the *Martinez*. At that time Hump finds fault with another passenger's irritation at the fog and its undue effect upon the ferry's progress:

> I felt quite amused at his unwarranted choler, and while he stumped indignantly up and down I fell to dwelling upon the romance of the fog. And romantic it certainly was—the fog, like the gray shadow of infinite mystery, brooding over the whirling speck of the earth. . . . (10)

For Hump, the fog, with it sense of mystery, reflects the dreamier side of his own nature; for Wolf, the reduced visibility represents a safe haven from his brother's ship. For both the fog serves as a place to hide from the coming age. That Hump's romantic musing in the fog on board the *Martinez* should be put to an end by a collision with a steamship seems appropriate. That the pilot of that same vessel should appear so emotionless at the moment of collision—

> he ran a calm and speculative eye over [the *Martinez*], as though to determine the precise point of the collision, and took no notice whatever when [her] pilot, white with rage, shouted, "Now you've done it!" (11)

—further accents the fact that the new era holds no place for Hump or Wolf, men who, whatever their shortcomings, are passionate about the ideas they espouse, and ill-fitted for a rational and reasoned world in which passion no longer has a place.

Wolf Larsen would rather run than confront the *Macedonia*, but more must be said about the dynamics of the conflict between the two sealers. Some might argue that Wolf and his men do physically challenge the men of the *Macedonia* when Larsen sends his hunters out to capture some of Death's men by force. The raid is successful. However, a number of qualifications are in order concerning this episode.

First, Wolf's men do not challenge the *Macedonia* outright, but attack her boats individually when they are spread out and far from the ship, when it is most safe to do so. In the sealing industry, individual boats, propelled by sail and oar, were often quite far from the main ship, and were often lost when they strayed too far to be found or were overtaken by bad weather (Busch, 133). Second, and more important, it is economic necessity that drives Wolf's men to attack the *Macedonia*'s crews, not Wolf's physical threats. The *Macedonia*, with her great speed and dependability, and her large number of boats, is a direct threat to the livelihood of all on board the *Ghost*:

> Having passed several miles behind our line of boats, the *Macedonia* proceeded to lower her own. We knew she carried fourteen boats to our five ... and she began dropping them far to leeward of our last boat, continued dropping them athwart our course, and finished dropping them far to windward of our first weather boat. The hunting, for us, was spoiled. There were no seals behind us, and ahead of us the line of fourteen boats, like a huge broom, swept the herd before it.... Each man felt that he had been robbed.... (London, 175)

Such an assault on the men is a literal threat to their lives, as Wolf makes clear: "Who steals my purse steals my right to live" (175).

For Wolf to utter such a statement negates the value he places on physical strength, since brute force alone no longer determines a man's survival. In the new age men must live by the purse, by their ability to accumulate capital, and in a capitalist society men are relieved of their purses every day by men physically weaker than them—men they often never see. Economics, not the threat of Wolf's physical strength, impels the *Ghost*'s hunters, at some risk to their lives, to catch hold of some of Death's men and press them into service on Wolf's ship. The economic reward to the men here is twofold. Not only do they improve their own chances by thinning out the hunters who travel ahead of them, but they are also promised "a dollar a skin for all the skins shot by our new hunters" (191).

In fact, when Wolf is finally overtaken by Death he is relieved of his crew not by violence, but economics. Death simply buys off Wolf's men:

> Hunters went back on me. He gave them a bigger lay. Heard him offering it. Did it right before me. Of course the crew gave me the

go-by. That was to be expected. All hands went over the side, and there I was, marooned on my own vessel. (238)

Wolf's physical strength, however prodigious, is of no use to him in his confrontations with the new era which Death and the *Macedonia* represent. When his incredible body and mind are later destroyed by the ravages of disease, the *Ghost* too is symbolically emasculated when the great masts, designed to stand against any storm (48), fall after their rigging is cut by one of the sailors leaving the ship. The *Ghost*, and with it the age of sail, is finished.

Some might argue that Hump's refitting of the *Ghost* on Endeavor Island, and his successful venture out to sea in her at the text's end, suggest that the age of sail, and all that it implies, is not yet finished, and that men like Hump and Wolf, creatures of intellect and passion, are not yet obsolete, that Darwinism and Romanticism both are alive and well at the text's close. To this objection, two final points will be made.

First, Hump's refitting of the *Ghost* is based less on physical strength (and not at all upon armchair idealizing) than upon the application of practical mechanical reasoning, on which the new era, that of Death and his like, is based. Hump succeeds in doing what no man could accomplish single-handedly only by employing a number of simple technologies, such as the shears and the windlass. Without the windlass, Hump could not complete his task at all. Wolf realizes this and attempts to destroy it. To his credit, Hump manages to repair the windlass but it is not easy. He is not a true soldier of the mechanical age:

Three days I worked on that windlass. Last of all things was I a mechanic, and in that time I accomplished what an ordinary machinist would have done in as many hours. I had to learn my tools to begin with, and every simple mechanical principle which such a man would have at his finger ends I had likewise to learn. (261)

Second, after making a successful bid for the open sea in the *Ghost*, Hump and Maud Brewster eventually spot a revenue cutter and are rescued by it. That they sight the cutter, a steamer, immediately upon burying Larsen at sea—"dragged down by the weight of iron" (283)—points to the final triumph of one era over another. The *Ghost*, crewless, is left abandoned on the swells, and Hump and Maud are carried back, or rather forward, to the world on a steamship. In the end, the *Macedonia*'s victory over the *Ghost* clearly

demonstrates the way in which both Humphrey Van Weyden *and* Wolf
Larsen embody ideas whose time has already passed.

BIBLIOGRAPHY

Anderson, Sherwood. *Winesburg, Ohio.* 1919. New York: Penguin, 1976.
Busch, Britton Cooper. *The War Against the Seal.* Kingston & Montreal: McGill-Queens
    University Press, 1985.
Carlson, Patricia Ann, ed. *Costerus 52.* Amsterdam: Rodopi, 1986.
Chapelle, Howard I. *The History of American Sailing Ships.* New York: Norton, 1935.
Foner, Phillip S., ed. *Jack London: American Rebel.* New York: Citadel, 1947.
London, Jack. *The Sea-Wolf.* 1904. New York: Signet, 1964.

PER SERRITSLEV PETERSEN

Jack London's Medusa of Truth

From the very start of his literary career, Jack London believed that a good fiction writer must also be a good thinker—that fictional authenticity and integrity must somehow be imbedded in philosophical authenticity and integrity. In his early essay "On the Writer's Philosophy of Life," and in his early letters to Cloudsley Johns, his intellectually "slovenly" friend (who also happened to share his literary ambitions and interests), London insists, again and again, on the proper philosophical foundation of the successful writer. This is how poor Cloudsley, who had previously been told to "get in and systematically ground [himself] in history, economics, biology and the kindred branches"[1] gets browbeaten by his self-appointed mentor and master, a veritable Jack of all trades, in a letter dated March 15, 1900: "To be well fitted for the tragedy of existence (intellectual existence), one must have a working philosophy, a synthesis of things. Have you a synthesis of things? Do you write, and talk, and build upon a foundation which you know is securely laid? Or do you not rather build with a hazy idea of 'to hell with the foundation.'" London then proceeds to catechize his friend on scientific principles such as the indestructibility of Matter, the persistence of Force, and the overall "dynamic principle, true of the metamorphosis of the universe"—principles that Cloudsley is urged to study "carefully and

From *Philosophy and Literature* 26, no. 1 (April 2002): 43–56. Copyright © 2002 by *Philosophy and Literature*.

painstakingly" before he can ever claim to have "a firm foundation for [his] philosophy of life" (*Letters*, pp. 170–71).

In London's admittedly heavy-handed *ad hominem* argument, one recognizes the philosophical sledgehammer of Ernest Everhard, the revolutionary hero of *The Iron Heel* and one of the fictional exponents of "that cold forbidding philosophy, materialistic monism,"[2] which also served as the scientific foundation of London's own philosophy of life. There are, however, not one, but *two* components to London's philosophy, which, as I shall argue in this essay, together constitute an essentially *dialectical* construction, a dynamic juxtaposition of and negotiation with, on the one hand, the "cold forbidding" Medusa of Truth and, on the other hand, the life-enhancing Aphrodite of Romance, the second of which is one of several versions of the vital Maia-Lie (Maia being the Buddhist term for the power that creates or re-creates the world as cosmic illusion).

Two points need to be stressed from the outset. First, London's work is *implicitly* aligned with *literary* naturalism—the "Zolaistic Movement" of modern American fiction that the genteel writer and editor Thomas Bailey Aldrich famously condemned for its "miasmatic breath"[3]—even though London himself would always qualify his own naturalism by insisting that, artistically, he was "an emotional materialist" (*Letters*, p. 329), and that his realism was, in the words of Martin Eden, one of his fictional alter egos, "an impassioned realism, shot through with human aspiration and faith."[4] Second, London's work is *explicitly* aligned with *philosophical* naturalism (as distinct from supernaturalism)—that is, naturalism as the philosophical or epistemological view that, to quote *The Oxford Companion to Philosophy* (1995), "everything is natural, i.e. that everything there is belongs to the world of nature, and so can be studied by the methods appropriate for studying that world." In philosophical practice, naturalism and materialism have tended to coalesce, materialism being basically understood as the view that everything is made of matter, which can be studied by the methods of natural science. Like London's philosophical alter ego Ernest Everhard (and also like fictional protagonists such as Wolf Larsen and Martin Eden), London declared himself "a materialistic monist," although, as he admitted to Cloudsley Johns, "there is dam little satisfaction in it." Rhetorically impersonating, as it were, Wolf Larsen, London, in the same letter, asks himself and his correspondent, "what squirming anywhere, damned or otherwise, means anything? That's the question I am always prone to put: What's this chemical ferment called life about? Small wonder that small men down the ages have conjured gods in answer. A little god is a snug little possession and explains it all. But how about you and me, who have no god?" (*Letters*, p. 270). Although there was "dam little satisfaction" in his naturalistic and materialistic philosophy, and although London did find ways of escaping from what Benjamin De Casseres, his Nietzschean philosopher-friend and literary protégé in New York, would refer to as the dreadful Medusa-Truth through various romantic-idealistic illusions (the Maya-Lie), London's intellectual conscience would always oblige him to return, eventually, to his philosophical Medusa-Truth—that is, Ernest Everhard's "cold forbidding philosophy, materialistic monism."

Intellectual conscience is used here with its Nietzschean connotations: in *The Gay Science*, Nietzsche notes that the great majority of people seems to lack an intellectual conscience in that they do not "consider it contemptible to believe this or that and to live accordingly, without having given themselves an account of the final and most certain reasons pro and con."[5] It is my contention that London belonged to that exclusive minority that could be said to possess an intellectual conscience, which explains why he had to come down so hard on his friend's "hazy idea of 'to hell with the [philosophical] foundation.'" It is also my contention that, throughout his life, London never really compromised his intellectual conscience—although he did play his own Maya games, Nietzsche's games of Gay Science (derived from the Provençal concept of *gaya scienza*, denoting the unity of singer, knight, and free spirit) when he felt the existential need to replace Medusa-Truth with Maya-Lie. Illusions, Henrik Ibsen's vital lies or Saul Bellow's ideal constructions (in *Dangling Man*) are, after all, necessary because man has become, to quote Nietzsche again, "a fantastic animal that has to fulfil one more condition than any other animal: man *has to* believe, to know, from time to time *why* he exists; his race cannot flourish without a periodic trust in life—without faith in *reason in life*" (*GS*, p. 75). By virtue of the Medusa-Maya dialectic, arguably a Nietzschean dialectic, London avoided compromising his intellectual conscience by submitting, for instance, to some kind of wholesale Jungian conversion into supernaturalism, as has been claimed first by his second wife Charmian in *The Book of Jack London* in 1921 and later by an increasing number of American academics. With no convincing textual evidence to the contrary, I must concur with Robert Barltrop's conclusion, in *Jack London: The Man, the Writer, the Rebel*, that London never "changed from the conviction he stated in a letter to Ralph Kasper, in 1914,"[6] that, as London asserts, "I am a hopeless materialist. I see the soul as nothing else than the sum of the activities of the organism plus personal habits, memories, experiences, of the organism, plus inherited habits, memories, experiences of the organism. *I believe that when I am dead, I am dead. I believe that with my death I am just as much obliterated as the last mosquito you or I smashed.*"[7]

In sum, London as philosopher 1) was a Nietzschean dialectician who mastered and negotiated the juxtaposition of conflicting ideas, perspectives, and values in life (the Medusa-Maya dichotomy being a crucial case in point);

and who consequently, 2) possessed philosophical authenticity and integrity, or what Nietzsche terms intellectual conscience. Now these contentions must appear highly questionable in contemporary American academe, seeing that very few London scholars or critics take the novelist's philosophy seriously. In *Jack London*, Earle Labor, the undisputed maestro among modern London scholars, describes London the philosopher as follows: "Self-educated, he considered himself a great thinker, yet he could unblinkingly accommodate to his *weltanschauung* the disparate philosophical attitudes of Friedrich Nietzsche, Karl Marx, Ernst Haeckel, Herbert Spencer, and Benjamin Kidd, while blandly admitting that metaphysicians like Ralph Waldo Emerson and Henri Bergson were beyond him."[8]

In his preface to *Jack London*, Labor notes that, in his efforts to avoid exaggerating the worth of his subject, he might actually have underestimated "the full magnitude of London's achievement" (p. 7). Certainly this is so with respect to London's philosophical achievement, but Labor is not alone among American academics in denigrating and trivializing London's philosophy. In *Male Call: Becoming Jack London*, Jonathan Auerbach proclaims that "attempts to make London a significant thinker strike [him] as . . . a bit ill-conceived," seeing that London was "inclined to indulge in philosophical speculation that frequently reveals on closer examination a fairly conventional grasp of Spencer, Darwin, Nietzsche, or Marx."[9] According to Auerbach's postmodernist thesis (the heuristic substance of which is encapsulated in the *male–mail* pun of the title), London's philosophy was not "primarily an abstracted or systematic way of thinking but something London would continually forge from his enormous intellectual energy and curiosity—to make himself—to make his person in print—cohere as a published writer" (p. 24).

Finally, London's philosophical achievement is most grievously misrepresented in Leonard Cassuto and Jeanne Campbell Reesman's introduction to *Rereading Jack London*: "Though London saw value and challenge in Nietzsche's ideas . . . we suggest that his unsystematic, often self-contradictory worldview, buttressed by his eccentric vision of 'individualistic socialism,' may better be described by Emersonian representativeness than by Nietzschean greatness and its accompanying discontents."[10] Cassuto and Reesman provide no textual evidence of London's "unsystematic, often self-contradictory world-view." Where, exactly, is it that London fails to integrate, say, Darwin, Marx, or Nietzsche in the dialectic of his working philosophy? Are all cases of philosophical eclecticism and perspectivism to be disqualified a priori as cases of intellectual incompetence? London must surely have turned in his grave when he saw himself nominated as one of Emerson's Representative Men. As Labor notes, Emerson's idiosyncratic transcendentalism was beyond London, as it was beyond Nietzsche, who lamented that "in Emerson we have *lost a philosopher.* . . . I do not know how much I would give if only I could bring it about, *ex post facto*, that such a glorious, great nature, rich in soul and spirit, might have gone through some *strict* discipline, a really scientific education" (*GS*, Intro., p. 7). However, if London would have declined his nomination for Representative Man, thus implicitly endorsing an Emersonian transcendentalism untrammelled by scientific education and discipline, London the dialectician would also, like his fictional alter ego Martin Eden, have disclaimed the title of Nietzschean superman, ironically characterizing himself as "a damn poor Nietzscheman" or "a fine Nietzsche-man . . . who [allows] his intellectual concepts to be shaken by the first sentiment or emotion that [strays] along— ay, to be shaken by the slave-morality itself" (*Martin Eden*, pp. 430, 402–3).

Though not a Nietzschean superman, London was a Nietzschean dialectician, playing the existential-philosophical games of Gay Science, that is, oscillating dialectically between the Medusa-Truth of his scientific naturalism and the Maya-Lie of his romantic idealism. It is within this philosophical scenario that London discovers the post-Nietzschean French philosopher Jules de Gaultier and appropriates, more or less explicitly, de Gaultier's philosophical argument and terminology for his later fictions, principally *The Mutiny of the Elsinore*, but also *John Barleycorn* and "The Red One," published in 1914, 1913, and 1918 respectively. De Gaultier is best known as the author of *Le Bovarysme*, and de Gaultier's philosophy of *bovarysme*, derived from the name and character of the eponymous heroine of Flaubert's *Madame Bovary*, became one of the minor philosophical crazes that swept Europe and America at the beginning of the twentieth century. T. S. Eliot, for instance, in "Shakespeare and the Stoicism of Seneca," diagnosed Othello's histrionic endgame as *bovarysme*, arguing that Othello "succeeds in turning himself into a pathetic figure, by adopting an *aesthetic* rather than a moral attitude, dramatizing himself against his environment." No writer, Eliot concluded, "has ever exposed this *bovarysme*, the human will to see things as they are not, more clearly than Shakespeare."[11] The human will or need to see oneself and things *as they are not*, or, in de Gaultier's own words, *se concevoir* or *s'imaginer autrement que l'on n'est*, to conceive or imagine oneself otherwise than one is, this is the philosophical and psychological core of *bovarysme*. In de Gaultier's post-Nietzschean philosophy, *bovarysme* is seen as a vital psychodynamic power in life, *le pouvoir d'imaginer*, and not as a moral weakness or flaw, as Eliot the Anglo-American Puritan would have it. In "*Madame Bovary*: The Cathedral and the Hospital" Harry Levin makes the same ideological mistake as Eliot, claiming that the "narcissistic attitude of Emma's, this self-hallucination induced by over-reading, this 'habit of conceiving ourselves otherwise than we are,' is so epidemic that Jules de Gaultier could diagnose the weakness of the modern mind as *Bovarysme*."[12]

London's use of *bovarysme* in *The Mutiny of the Elsinore*, however, is philosophically authentic. It is the protagonist Pathurst, another fictional London alter ego, who articulates and celebrates de Gaultier's philosophy in the book. Pathurst himself is a successful but blasé and ennuyé thirty-year-old writer, for whom life and women have lost their savor because he has "reached an intellectual and artistic climacteric, a life-climacteric of some sort" (p. 57). *Happiness, however, is a woman*, as Zarathustra famously spoke,[13] and, in London's masculine romance, Pathurst is predestined to fall in love with the glorious Miss West, the captain's daughter on board the *Elsinore*, a full-bodied, red-blooded superwoman, the female incarnation of the "cosmic sap" (p. 55) and the "ruthless passion for life, always life, more life on the planet" (p. 55). A significant part of Pathurst and Miss West's maritime courtship is taken up with "discussing philosophy and art, while a few feet away from [them], on this tiny floating world, all the grimy, sordid tragedy of sordid, malformed, brutish life plays itself out" (p. 143). As in the earlier sea-romance *The Sea-Wolf* (1904), which includes the ongoing philosophical battle between Wolf Larsen's naturalism/materialism and Humphrey Van Weyden's idealism/romanticism, London also *philosophizes* his sea-romance in *The Mutiny of the Elsinore* (no one is ever going to accuse *him* of intellectual naivete). London's philosophy of romance, expounded by Pathurst in the novel, turns out to be de Gaultier's *bovarysme* gleaned from a philosophical symposium featuring Pathurst's Jewish New York friend, Ben De Casseres, evidently the American authority on de Gaultier's philosophy. According to De Casseres, whose argument Pathurst repeats partly to Miss West, partly to himself, de Gaultier's philosophical genealogy can be traced back to Schopenhauer and Nietzsche, but out of Schopenhauer's and Nietzsche's philosophical formulas de Gaultier has constructed an even profounder formula: "The 'Will-to-Live' of the one and the 'Will-to-Power' of the other were, after all, only parts of de Gaultier's supreme generalization, the 'Will-to-Illusion'" (p. 113). A few pages later, Pathurst, who has somehow managed to memorize verbatim De Casseres's eloquent version/translation of de Gaultier's Will-to-Illusion philosophy, which was presented "over the wine in Mouquin's [restaurant]," reproduces this speech:

The profoundest instinct in man is to war against the truth; that is, against the Real. He shuns facts from his infancy. His life is a perpetual evasion. Miracle, chimera and to-morrow keep him alive. He lives on fiction and myth. It is the Lie that makes him free. Animals alone are given the privilege of lifting the veil of Isis; men dare not. The animal, awake, has no fictional escape from the Real because he has no imagination. Man, awake, is compelled to seek a perpetual escape into Hope, Belief, Fable, Art, God, Socialism, Immortality, Alcohol, Love. From Medusa-Truth he makes appeal to Maya-Lie. (p. 121)

Pathurst concludes his lecture on *bovarysme* by boasting that "Ben will agree that I have quoted him fairly" (p. 121).

Perhaps it is time now to expose London's intertextual hoax: Pathurst/ London did not quote De Casseres from memory (a phenomenal memory, if that was the case), but from a copy of De Casseres's essay "Jules de Gaultier: Super-Nietzschean."[14] The fictional De Casseres is identical with the American journalist, writer and poet Benjamin De Casseres, whom London met in New York after he had read the former's poem "Prelude." In a letter to De Casseres, dated February 12, 1912, London praises "Prelude" as "the poetry of utter philosophy," and "the quintessence of stinging philosophy put into stinging phrases" (*Letters*, p. 1,067). London was genuinely impressed by De Casseres, whom he characterized as "really and truly the American Nietzsche" in a letter to his publisher George P. Brett, adding, however, the following rather ambiguous *obiter dictum*: "I, as you know, am in the opposite intellectual camp. Yet no man in my own camp stirs me as does Nietzsche or as does De Casseres" (*Letters*, p. 1,072).[15] London must have been an avid reader of De Casseres's philosophical essays—a collection of which was published in 1926 as *Forty Immortals*[16]—and Pathurst's engagement in de Gaultier's philosophy in *The Mutiny of the Elsinore* suggests that London endorsed De Casseres's high opinion of de Gaultier. Indeed, in "Jules De Gaultier: The Prospero of Philosophy," De Casseres acclaimed de Gaultier as the modern Prospero of Thought, the "Frenchman who has climbed higher than either Schopenhauer and [sic] Nietzsche."[17]

But how can London's philosophical endorsement of de Gaultier's *bovarysme* possibly be accommodated, to use Labor's phrase, to his intellectually conscientious philosophical naturalism? Is London, after all, lacking in philosophical authenticity and integrity and encumbered thus by an "unsystematic, often self-contradictory worldview"? The answer is still *no*: only by failing to appreciate London's basically *dialectical* argument, his mastery and negotiation of juxtaposed, conflicting ideas, perspectives, and values in life, can one reach any other conclusion. The existential conflict between the Medusa-Truth and the Maya-Lie, in fact, had been diagnosed and articulated by London from the very beginning of his literary career or, in London's own phrase, "intellectual existence." The discovery of de Gaultier's *bovarysme* through De Casseres undoubtedly triggered a kind of eureka response in London, as did De Casseres's philosophical radicalism in general. Witness London's enthusiasm in his first letter to De Casseres in New York where he suggests a meeting after theatre-time: "We ought to have a hell of a lot to say to each other" (*Letters*, p. 1,067).

In *The Mutiny of the Elsinore*, Pathurst is the world-weary victim of Medusa-Truth, an enlightened nihilist, whom, like Hamlet, man delights not, nor woman either; if he is to escape the suicidal fate of a Martin Eden (another writer-turned-radical-nihilist in London's fiction), he must, philosophically, opt for the Will-to-Illusion—he must make an appeal to Maya-Lie because man cannot, in Nietzsche's words, "flourish without a periodic trust in life—without faith in *reason in life*." In Pathurst's case, the vital lie or illusion is Love, the Aphrodite of Romance who opposes the Medusa of Truth. Pathurst self-consciously turns *bovaryste*, falls in love with Miss West, and flourishes with a vengeance:

> I have achieved what my very philosophy tells me is the greatest achievement a man can make. I have found the love of woman. . . . Love is the final word. To the rational it alone gives the super-rational sanction for living. Like Bergson in his overhanging heaven of intuition, or like one who has bathed in Pentecostal fire and seen the New Jerusalem, so I have trod the materialistic dictums of science underfoot, scaled the last peak of philosophy, and leaped into my heaven, which, after all, is within myself. (pp. 244–45)

Psychobiographically, Pathurst's conception of love as secularized, individualized religion (his heaven is *within himself*) corresponds closely with London's expressions of passion for Charmian Kittredge: "Our love small! Dear, it might be small did the love of God enter into my heart, and the belief in an eternity of living and an eternity of the unguessed joys of Paradise. But remember my philosophy of life & death, and see clearly how much my love for you & your love for me must mean to me. Ah Love, it looms large. It fills my whole horizon" (*Letters*, p. 390).

Most interesting, however, is Pathurst's interpretation of his transformation as a *philosophical achievement*, for London's preoccupation with dialectical oscillation in the modern psyche—between scientific rationality and ecstatic or transcendent superrationality, between de Gaultier's Medusa-Truth and Maya-Lie—can be traced back to the very beginning of his career as a writer. We find this motif, loud and clear, in the philosophical debate between Wace, the melancholy "Werther of science," and Kempton, the "overcivilized, decadent dreamer" in *The Kempton-Wace Letters* (p. 125).[18] In Kempton's words, "We live most when we love most. The love of romance and the romance of love is the only coin for which the heart-hurt sell their death. A trick? Perhaps. The love of life is a trick to save the races from self-murder" (p. 157). The same dialectical oscillation informs the motif of transcendence in London's famous description, in *The Call of the Wild*, of the ecstasy that epitomizes Buck's supercanine consummation, the "ecstasy that marks the summit of life and beyond which life cannot rise," the ecstasy that "comes when one is most alive, and . . . as a complete forgetfulness that one is alive" (pp. 76–77).

In *The Sea-Wolf*, published a year after *The Kempton-Wace Letters* and *The Call of the Wild* in 1904, London enacts the conflict between the Medusa of Truth and the Aphrodite of Romance in the philosophical confrontation between Wolf Larsen, a brutalized or demonized version of the melancholy Werther of Science, and the two idealists and romantic lovers held prisoners on board his ship, Humphrey Van Weyden and Maud Brewster—two "sentimentalists," to quote Wolf Larsen, "really and truly happy at dreaming and finding things good." Their feeling of happiness, Wolf Larsen notes, is merely "a sentiment, a something based upon illusion and not a product of the intellect at all" (p. 173). Still, even Wolf Larsen cannot help yearning to turn *bovaryste* to escape from the Medusa-Truth and make his appeal to Maya-Lie because, "after all, delight is the wage for living" (p. 174). What prevents Wolf Larsen from making his leap into the heaven of illusions is, of course, his intellectual conscience, and the price he has to pay for that conscience is the "old primal melancholy" (p. 174), "sadness as the penalty which the materialist ever pays for his materialism" (p. 175).

One of London's protagonists, Ernest Everhard in *The Iron Heel*, has no less than three opportunities to cure himself of "that cold and forbidding philosophy of materialistic monism," and is saved by De Casseres's Maya-Lies of Hope, Socialism, and Love respectively. But not all are so lucky. The eponymous protagonist of *Martin Eden*, published only a year after *Heel* in 1909, is a hard-core Nietzschean individualist, so Socialism is not an option for him. But then Love, the Aphrodite of Romance, promises to be Martin's saving illusion:

> Love [Martin reflects] was the most exalted expression of life. Nature had been busy designing him, as she had been busy with all normal men, for the purpose of loving. She had spent ten thousand centuries—ay, a hundred thousand and a million centuries upon the task, and he was the best she could do. She had made love the strongest thing in him, increased its power a myriad per cent with her gift of imagination, and sent him forth into the ephemera to thrill and melt and mate. (pp. 381–82)

Alas, Ruth, the woman Martin has picked as his Aphrodite, proves to be exactly what his friend Brissenden had warned him of, namely "the pusillanimous product of bourgeois-sheltered life" (p. 346). At the instigation of her bourgeois family, pusillanimous Ruth breaks off the engagement. Confronting anew the Medusa of Truth, the disillusioned Martin accepts her scientific diagnosis: "It was an idealized Ruth that he had loved, an ethereal creature of his own creating, the bright and luminous spirit of his love-poems. The real bourgeois Ruth, with all the bourgeois failings, and with the hopeless cramp of bourgeois psychology in her mind, he had never loved" (pp. 463–64). Left in an existential limbo, Martin commits suicide by drowning himself en route to the South Seas, which might have served as another saving illusion. But after the Medusa of Truth has ousted the Aphrodite of Romance, the South Seas "charmed him no more than did bourgeois civilization" (p. 474).

London realizes the Medusa of Truth in her most nightmarish proportions in *John Barleycorn*. White Logic, a figure that shares the original Medusa's monstrosity and fatality, is "the ardent messenger of truth beyond truth, the antithesis of life, cruel and bleak as interstellar space, pulseless and frozen as absolute zero, dazzling with the frost of irrefragable logic and unforgettable fact" (p. 188). The philosophical argument of these so-called alcoholic memoirs can be summarized as follows. As long as one believes in "the whole host of fond illusions that keep the world turning around" (p. 135), there is no need or desire for alcohol, personified by John Barleycorn, but when one loses these vital illusions by making "the ancient mistake of pursuing Truth too relentlessly," by reading, for instance, "too much positive science," one may fall victim to the "long sickness of pessimism" (p. 155) and may need John Barleycorn as an anodyne. But soon one learns that White Logic is John Barleycorn's intimate companion; in the long run, alcoholism will only exacerbate the pessimism and nihilism that John Barleycorn was intended to cure in the first place. White Logic whispers, "I am truth. You know it. You cannot combat me. They say I make for death. What of it? It is truth. Life lies in order to live. Life is a perpetual *lie-telling* process" (p. 192).

London started writing *John Barleycorn* in August 1912, and the rhetoric in which White Logic's anti-*bovaryste* argument is couched, reflects, albeit ironically, London's fascination with de Gaultier's philosophy as expounded by De Casseres (*Letters*, p. 1,079). White Logic jeers at the "sense-drunk" *bovaryste*, whose stupid "brain is filled with superrational sanctions and obsessions" (p. 193), and whose "ideal of happiness [must be] a jelly-like organism floating in a tideless, tepid, twilight sea. . . . One step removed," White Logic clinches his diabolic argument, "from the annihilating bliss of Buddha's Nirvana" (p. 194). As in the case of Ernest Everhard, it is Socialism, "his one remaining illusion—the PEOPLE" (p. 134), and Love, "the love of woman to complete the cure and lull [his] pessimism asleep" (p. 157) that save the narrator-protagonist of London's alcoholic romance from the clutches of the Medusa of Truth in the guise of White Logic.

The textual and philosophical genealogy of London's Medusa of Truth has, I believe, now been accounted for. The Medusa metaphor first appears in Benjamin De Casseres's "Jules de Gaultier: Super-Nietzschean" (1913), as Medusa-Truth in dialectical opposition to Maya-Lie, the crucial psychodynamic agency of de Gaultier's *bovarysme*. In London's *The Mutiny of the Elsinore*, the Medusa of Truth appears in the intertextually appropriated De Casseres quotation. Although London only once refers to this *femme fatale* in his own authentic discourse, what a majestic appearance when she arrives at the very end of one of London's last and most haunting stories, "The Red One," where Bassett, the dying scientist-protagonist ends up gazing upon "the serene face of the Medusa, Truth" (p. 211). This story, especially its ending, has been misread by an increasing number of academic critics who overlook London's consistently dialectical philosophy of life. Recently, for instance, in "The Myth of Hope in Jack London's 'The Red One,'" Lawrence I. Berkove virtually rewrites London's story, claiming that the "overt allusion to Medusa . . . is deceptive—self-deceptive, actually—on Bassett's part," and that "[Bassett's] error is signaled by his peculiar identification of Medusa with truth" (in Cassuto and Reesman, p. 212). Berkove concludes that, for London, Bassett exemplifies "a man who confuses wisdom for truth, who looks upon Medusa instead of Athena," because, as he explains, in Greek mythology Perseus killed Medusa with Athena's help (p. 213). Throughout the text, in fact, London foregrounds Bassett's dialectical oscillation between scientific truth and utopian romance, between Medusa and Maya—the latter being epitomized by the science-fictionally engineered transcendence of the Red One, the "wonderful messenger, winged with intelligence across space" (p. 206), containing, within its perfect sphere, "the speech and wisdom of the stars" (p. 207). (There is, incidentally, no Aphrodite of Romance in this story, the only female in Bassett's Melanesian adventure being the bushwoman Balatta, "as unbeautiful a prototype of woman as he, with a scientist's eye, had ever gazed upon" [p. 196].) A split second before the serene face of Medusa appears, while he is awaiting the bite of Ngurn the "devil-devil" priest's razor-edged hatchet, Bassett experiences, in the ecstasy at the Red One's "abrupt and thunderous liberation of sound" (p. 210), a vision of "the Unknown, a sense of impending marvel of the rending of walls before the imaginable" (p. 211). From the very beginning, the Red One has been associated with this *imaginable*, de Gaultier's *pouvoir d'imaginer*. Although Bassett claims to be "a scientist first, a humanist afterward" (p. 202), he also proves to be an all-too-human *bovaryste* with a yearning for Hope, a Nietzschean "faith in *reason in life*," and this hope and faith Bassett *le bovaryste* projects into the Red One, "invested," as it is by the dying man's feverish imagination, "with the intelligence of supermen of planets of other suns" (p. 210).

But crucially, the last swing of Bassett's dialectical pendulum returns him to the Medusa of Truth—that is, scientism, rationalism, naturalism, Nietzsche's radical nihilism, "the Horror, the Horror" of Joseph Conrad's and Western modernity's Heart of Darkness, and the philosophical core of London's modernist "tragedy of existence (intellectual existence)." At the end of "The Red One," Bassett's intellectual conscience strikes back once more, a point ignored by Jungian readers of the story.[19] Exit *tout bovarysme*: the reader is left with Bassett's ghoulish "vision of his head turning slowly, always turning, in the devil-devil house beside the breadfruit tree" (p. 211).

NOTES

1. *The Letters of Jack London*, ed. Earle Labor, Robert C. Leitz III, and Milo Shepard, 3 vols. (Stanford: Stanford University Press, 1988), p. 125.

2. Jack London, *The Iron Heel* (1907; reprint, London: Journeyman Press, 1980), p. 116.

3. Quoted in *American Realism and Naturalism: Howells to London*, ed. Donald Pizer (Cambridge: Cambridge University Press, 1995), p. 40.

4. Jack London, *Martin Eden* (1909; reprint, Harmondsworth: Penguin, 1984), p. 283.

5. Friedrich Nietzsche, *The Gay Science*, trans. Walter Kaufmann (1882; reprint, New York: Random House, 1974), p. 76. London's writing, fictional or otherwise, is impregnated with Nietzschean philosophy and references to Nietzsche. London had begun a more systematic reading of Nietzsche's work in 1904, and, in a letter from the following year, he mentions his "Nietzsche sickness," that is, what Nietzsche himself terms radical nihilism, from which London claims he has just emerged, enclosing, by way of explanation, the passage from *Thus Spoke Zarathustra*, where Zarathustra enjoins man to break the Christian tables of the good and embarks him on his high modernist sea, thus exposing him to "the great terror, the great outlook, the great sickness, the great nausea" (*Letters*, p. 500).

6. Robert Barltrop, *Jack London: the Man, the Writer, the Rebel* (London: Pluto Press, 1976), p. 174.

7. The next paragraph in the letter, which Barltrop leaves out, is, I think, worth quoting in full as a summation of London's philosophical self-diagnosis: "I have no patience with fly-by-night philosophers such as Bergson. I have no patience with the metaphysical philosophers. With them, always, the wish is parent to the thought, and their wish is parent to their profoundest philosophical conclusions. I join with Haeckel in being what, in lieu of any other phrase, I am compelled to call 'a positive scientific thinker'" (*Letters*, p. 1,339).

8. Earle Labor, *Jack London* (New York: Twayne, 1974), pp. 20–21.

9. Jonathan Auerbach, *Male Call: Becoming Jack London* (Durham: Duke University Press, 1996), p. 3.

10. *Rereading Jack London*, ed. Leonard Cassuto and Jeanne Campbell Reesman (Stanford: Stanford University Press, 1996), pp. 3–4.

11. T. S. Eliot, *Selected Essays* (London: Faber and Faber, 1961), pp. 130–31.

12. Harry Levin, "*Madame Bovary*: The Cathedral and the Hospital," reprinted in *Madame Bovary* (New York: Norton, 1965), p. 409.

13. Friedrich Nietzsche, *Thus Spoke Zarathustra*, trans. R. J. Hollingdale (Harmondsworth: Penguin, 1969), p. 184.

14. Benjamin De Casseres, "Jules de Gaultier: Super-Nietszchean," *The Forum* 49 (January 1913): 86–90.

15. London's statement reflects his concern for public relations and political correctness: his American reading public might just stomach his socialism, but *not* his atheistic Nietzscheanism.

16. Benjamin De Casseres, *Forty Immortals* (New York: Seven Arts, 1926).

17. Benjamin De Casseres, "Jules de Gaultier: The Prospero of Philosophy," *Reedy's Mirror* (1915): 172.

18. Subsequent references to London's work cite the following editions: *The Kempton-Wace Letters* (New York: Macmillan, 1903); *The Call of the Wild, White Fang, and Other Stories* (1903; reprint, Harmondsworth: Penguin, 1981); *The Sea-Wolf and Other Stories* (1904; reprint, Harmondsworth: Penguin, 1989); *John Barleycorn* (Oxford: Oxford University Press, 1992); "The Red One," *The Science Fiction Stories of Jack London* (New York: Citadel Press, 1993).

19. See, for instance, Clarice Stacz's Jungian interpretation of the story, complete with a holistically happy ending, in *American Dreamers* (New York: St. Martin's Press, 1988), p. 312.

LISA HOPKINS

Jack London's Evolutionary Hierarchies: Dogs, Wolves, and Men

When Jack London published *The Call of the Wild* in 1903, and followed it up with its quasi-sequel *White Fang* in 1906, he was touching directly on a theme that was and has remained highly controversial in American culture: evolution. Behind these apparently innocent, heroic, and quasi-Aesopian fables, with their mythopoeic nomenclature, lie profound concerns with changes in animal nature over time. Moreover, London's intricate interweaving of the stories of Buck and White Fang with those of their human masters does more than demonstrate his firm belief in environmental determinism; it also suggests that what is true of animals may be so of humans too. This connection was made early in the reception of the novels, and the developmental extremes of which Buck and White Fang ultimately prove capable led to London being often criticized (most notably perhaps by Theodore Roosevelt) for anthropomorphizing and sentimentalizing his canine creations. Though London certainly does draw parallels between animal and human behavior—as one would indeed expect from one committed to evolutionary theory—what seems to me much more striking are in fact the *differences* between his dogs and his men and what these may imply about London's understanding and use of the vexed differentiations between species and race.

From *Evolution and Eugenics in American Literature and Culture, 1880–1940: Essays on Ideological Conflict and Complicity*, edited and with an introduction by Lois A. Cuddy and Claire M. Roche, pp. 89–101. Published by Bucknell University Press. Copyright © 2003 by Rosemont Publishing and Printing.

Though both Buck and White Fang change dramatically during the course of their respective narratives, the human beings with whom they have to deal remain remarkably constant. John Thornton in *The Call of the Wild* and Weedon Scott in *White Fang* are always essentially good and deserving; Jim Hall, although actually innocent of the crime for which Judge Scott sentenced him, was nevertheless a bad lot in general, as his two previous convictions showed, and has not improved in prison. Contrary to Judge Scott's predictions, you *can* cure a chicken-killing dog, but human beings seem inherently recidivist. Similarly, Leclère in the short story "Bâtard" starts vicious and remains so. Indeed London makes much play of dogs' alleged ability to read human character instinctively and unerringly: White Fang may not know his own mother again, but although he has never heard of Jim Hall and knows nothing of his reasons for seeking revenge on Judge Scott, he immediately recognizes his felonious intent. London's dogs may learn and change, but his men, it seems, are what they are.

To some extent the reason is, as London constantly reminds us, that there are always two modes of being available to dogs. Humans may, as we now know, share 98 percent of their genes with chimpanzees, but we do not form part of the same breeding group; speciation has definitively and apparently irrevocably taken place. Dogs, by contrast, remain much closer to wolves and, crucially, can still interbreed with them. Indeed, White Fang is the product of precisely such a mating and is ultimately acclaimed by the Scotts as a "Blessed Wolf." So incomplete does the process of speciation seem to be that an individual animal is capable of effectively fast-tracking in its own person the entire history of the process.

This echoes the popular mid-nineteenth century idea that the development of the human embryo recapitulated that of the entire species, progressing from an initially reptilian form to an ultimately mammalian one. Adult humans, however, lack this fluidity. Though the discovery of Neanderthal man in 1856 had made it plain that there had once been species of hominids other than *Homo sapiens*, none survived (and the extent to which interbreeding had ever been possible continues to be debated). Man could not, in his own person, ever change his behavior so markedly as to find himself reclassified from one species to another as do both Buck and White Fang.

Even for dogs, however, the process is not fully two-way. After the death of Jack Thornton, Buck answers the call of the wild finally and irrevocably, not only running with the wild brother but actually heading the wolf pack. White Fang, however, is ultimately praised by the Scotts precisely for his retention of the characteristics of a wolf despite his assimilation into the family and the law. Although development in both directions is equally possible, it is clear that one has greater cachet, and is certainly better calculated to appeal to a writer like London, who had made his reputation through his own reputed closeness to the wild, as manifested in his oyster piracy and his Klondike and "Northland" trips. Indeed perhaps London's ultimate evolutionary fantasy would be a human being who could answer the call of the wild as effectively as a dog.

And this is, I think, what he did in fact fantasize in *Before Adam*, the work that followed *White Fang*. Like *White Fang*, *Before Adam* was written in little more than a month, having clearly caught its writer's imagination. Like *White Fang*, too, it was initially serialized, allowing for an episodic narrative method that essentially boils down to construction-by-cliffhanger. There are also significant differences, though, and one of the most striking is that unlike both *White Fang* and *The Call of the Wild*, *Before Adam* is set in the past, not the present. This shift inherently qualifies and indeed arguably even vitiates the entire issue of progression—in whichever direction—that lies at the thematic core of the dog books. But if London has set himself one problem, he has solved another. Thus, I want to argue that here, as in the Northland stories, he has found in race a classeme for men that he finds equivalent to that of speciation in dogs, and that it is indeed the sensitivities inevitably attendant on race issues that complicate his treatment of progression. (I use the word "men" advisedly, for though the exchange of Indian women facilitates the developmental trajectory of London's white heroes, the women themselves remain static counters in the transaction.)

London's theories of race were complex. Though he is notorious for his alleged remark "What the devil! I am first of all a white man and only then a Socialist" (Foner 1947, 59), Jonathan Auerbach points out that miscegenation and flexibility of identity were both crucial parts of his ideas about race (Auerbach 1996, 58). Maxwell Geismar similarly argues that "the vicious tone of London's theories of racial supremacy applied mainly, as it were, to *poor* Negroes—Negroes or the other 'inferior races' who were inferior precisely because they had not as yet acquired breeding, wealth or social tradition" (Geismar 1954, 214). For London, racial classifications are in flux, and not only can reclassification be in some sense earned, but contact with the nonwhite also identifies and indeed defines the values of whiteness. Thus though London's men may not be able to choose between being dog or wolf, they can move between modes of being. London instantiates this condition as a reified and mythologized redness and whiteness with the Indian not only standing to the white man as the wolf does to the dog, but also, and more importantly for London's purposes, facilitating the transition of white man to the condition of the wolf.

London's representations of race and ethnicity are conditioned by more than his theories about Native Americans, however. The "Kipling of the

Klondike" seems also to have been very aware of the extent to which he was negotiating literary territory explored by British rather than American writers. The three authors he is known to have read in the Klondike—Darwin, Milton, and Kipling—not only dealt in various ways with the question of human origins and nature, but also either participated in or provided crucial ideological ammunition for the British imperial adventure. London, therefore, does not only chart the difference between the evolution of men and dogs, he also negotiates the related ideological terrain of the evolution of ideas about evolution, and his own difference from the imperially-inflected models of his British comparators. Here, his commitment to the influence of environment does double duty because he is able to suggest that locale—in particular the Northland—plays a crucial part in facilitating a less deterministic and teleologically-oriented model than that traditionally found in British accounts of evolution.

London himself called *The Call of the Wild* a portrait of "devolution or decivilization of a dog" and *White Fang* "the evolution, the civilization of a dog—development of domesticity, faithfulness, love, morality, and all the amenities and virtues." London's view of evolution here is distinctly different from the classic Darwinian account, for he goes on to remark that "I am an evolutionist, therefore a broad optimist . . . my love for the human (in the slime though he be) comes from my knowing him as he is and seeing the divine possibilities ahead of him. That's the whole motive of my 'White Fang'" (1990, xv). Darwin's disavowal of a direction or teleology for evolutionary processes had disabled any such possibility of optimism in his own works. London's theories, however, permit of astonishing extremes of development. Initially White Fang has an "outlook [that] was bleak and materialistic. The world as he saw it was a fierce and brutal world, a world without warmth, a world in which caresses and affection and the bright sweetness of the spirit did not exist" (192). However, it was London's creed that "Every atom of organic life is plastic. . . . Let the pressure be one way and we have atavism . . . the other the domestication, civilization. I have always been impressed with the awful plasticity of life and I feel that I can never lay enough stress upon the marvelous power and influence of environment" (xv), and that "every atom" applies to mental and spiritual as much as to physical makeup. Thus White Fang develops not only physically, becoming "quicker of movement than the other dogs, swifter of foot, craftier, deadlier, more lithe, more lean with iron-like muscle and sinew, more enduring, more cruel, more ferocious, and more intelligent" (182), but also mentally, learning to appreciate that although Weedon Scott may be physically weaker than the roughnecks, they recognize his social superiority and keep their hands off him. In White Fang's perceptions, "As the days went by, the evolution of *like* into *love* was accelerated" (249).

In this view of evolution as a potentially two-way process and the concomitant lack of emphasis on fixed class-stratification, London differs very notably from his British contemporaries. Conan Doyle's *Hound of the Baskervilles*, for instance, also centers on a dog, albeit to very different effect, and also registers a considerable interest in evolution and heredity, as might indeed be expected from its medically-trained author. But Conan Doyle differs markedly from London in his insistence on the narrative as illustrating the working-out of a divine plan (Conan Doyle 1996, 18). This difference of emphasis is the primary result of comparing London with Conan Doyle's friend and contemporary, Rider Haggard. Very like Haggard in his own great personal interest in agriculture, London differed from him profoundly in his belief in the possibility of change and improvement, whereas the fatalistic Haggard stressed continuity.[1] Moreover, the two men are also sharply differentiated in their attitudes about the question of an overall purpose in the universe. Haggard certainly makes copious use in his writings of the trappings of evolutionary theory. However, as the concluding lines of the poem that appears on the title page of *Allan and the Ice-Gods* (1971) reminds us, there may be more than one explanation of events, and we cannot be sure which is the true one. "Some call it Evolution, / And others call it God," says Carruth. The novel itself opens with a similar debate by Allan Quatermain before he meets a palaeolithic version of himself. This tribe worships a frozen mammoth and lives by "the doctrine of the survival of the fittest and the rights of the strong over the weak, as Nature preaches them in all her workings" (Haggard 1971, 74).

Indeed both *Allan and the Ice-Gods* and *The Ancient Allan* (1920) look almost like a direct riposte to London. In the former, Allan Quatermain reexperiences his past as palaeolithic man; in the second, he recalls himself as "half human," as "black man," and as Egyptian of Ethiopian descent. Both thus come very close to *Before Adam* (1907), and *Allan and the Ice-Gods* in particular shares with *Before Adam* descriptions of the advance of ice to a place where it had not previously been seen and a sense of the resulting molding of the landscape by glaciation. Furthermore, linking these two works are accounts of attack by seaborne invaders, the hero's challenging of a huge and dominant leader who monopolizes the supply of women, and crucial plot developments motivated by the love of a woman from outside the tribe.

There are, however, striking and very significant differences. Haggard, whose already nascent interest in spiritualism was much intensified after the early death of his beloved only son, constantly insists both on the workings of a divine plan and on the persistence of individual human identities across gaps of time and after death. Though Allan Quatermain may have had another name in his earlier incarnations, he is always recognizably himself, and finds that his destiny is always inextricably interwoven with the same

small, tight-knit group of people. London's protagonist, in contrast, is identified only by a soubriquet in his avatar and has no name or other identifying
features in his modern descendant. (Indeed the possibility that the novel is
autobiographical is left titillatingly open, and critics of London have not been
slow to point to the parallels between London's own illegitimacy and Big
Tooth's ignorance of the eventual fate of his father. Moreover, the elusiveness
of the Swift One certainly has something in common with the alleged behavior of London's second wife, Charmian Kittredge.) Yet, apart from dreams,
the novel seems to contest the idea of continuity between the modern world
and the primeval. The only point of contact between his otherwise entirely
severed and discontinuous lives is a resemblance between Marrow-Bone and
his father's gardener, which seems primarily attributable to the fact that both
are old.

Haggard is also invariably at pains to stress that the ancient Allan was
just as inventive and ingenious as the modern one (and just as fine a shot, even
though his weapons were different). The narrator of *Before Adam*, by contrast,
records that Big Tooth and the Folk "were without weapons, without fire, and
in the raw beginnings of speech. The device of writing lay so far in the future
that I am appalled when I think of it" (8: 2);[2] similarly, "Our evolution into
cooking animals lay in the tight-rolled scroll of the future" (8: 5). The narrator
repeatedly stresses that they show no initiative or constancy of purpose, and
their only discoveries and advances are made entirely by accident—indeed
London remarked that he wrote the book specifically to show "that in a single
generation the only device primitive man, in my story, invented, was the carrying of water and berries in gourds" (Labor 1974, 106). Not without reason
does London's narrator observe, "As I look back I see clearly how our lives
and destinies are shaped by the merest chance" (*Before Adam*, 12: 3). Although
Buck in *The Call of the Wild* has race memories of times with a caveman,
"shorter of leg and longer of arm, with muscles that were stringy and knotty
rather than rounded and swelling" (41), Big Tooth and the Folk have not yet
reached even that stage of incipient civilization. There are no dogs in this
novel except for the wild ones that chase Big Tooth up the cliff and almost eat
him (12: 1) and the puppy that Big Tooth attempts to tame but which Lop-
Ear eats, an episode that the narrator uses to stress yet again the workings of
chance rather than design: "[t]o show you how fortuitous was development
in those days let me state that had it not been for the gluttony of Lop-Ear
I might have brought about the domestication of the dog" (8: 3). London's
early men learn nothing so fast as do either Buck or White Fang.

The most notable difference from Haggard, however, is that London
specifically denies (in *Before Adam*, at any rate)[3] that the phenomenon he is
describing is reincarnation:

I do believe that it is the possession of this other-personality—but not so strong a one as mine—that has in some few others given rise to belief in personal reincarnation experiences. It is very plausible to such people, a most convincing hypothesis. When they have visions of scenes they have never seen in the flesh, memories of acts and events dating back in time, the simplest explanation is that they have lived before. . . . But they are wrong. It is not reincarnation. I have visions of myself roaming through the forests of the Younger World; and yet it is not myself that I see but one that is only remotely a part of me, as my father and grandfather are parts of me less remote. (2:2)

Haggard unequivocally accepts the idea of reincarnation, and even Conan Doyle flirts with it, making Holmes say in *The Hound of the Baskervilles* that "A study of family portraits is enough to convert a man to the doctrine of reincarnation" (145). London's narrative, however, even questions and problematizes the very possibility of the relationship between the narrator and his "other-self," as he calls Big Tooth.

One of the most remarkable features of *Before Adam* is the way in which it repeatedly insists on the lack of success of its protagonist's people: "We were the first of the Folk to set foot on the north bank of the river, and, for that matter, I believe the last. That they would have done so in the time to come is undoubted; but the migration of the Fire People, and the consequent migration of the survivors of the Folk, set back our evolution for centuries" (11: 4). Like discourses of degeneration, London stresses the dark side of evolution; his narrative consistently frustrates any sense of progression and dwells instead on failure. The Folk as we know them during the course of the story are, ultimately, completely wiped out. Red-Eye survives, but reverts to the Tree People, to whom he had always seemed more properly to belong. Big Tooth himself survives, but he had not originally been part of the Folk. We are also explicitly told that the characteristics of his parents seem not in any sense to have been passed down: his mother "was like a large orangutan, . . . or like a chimpanzee, and yet, in sharp and definite ways, quite different" (3: 2), which does not sound even like Bigfoot himself, while his father "seemed half man, and half ape, and yet not ape, and not yet man. . . . There is nothing like him to-day on the earth, under the earth, nor in the earth" (3: 3).

Big Tooth's modern descendant wonders about the chain of descent:

I, the modern, am incontestably a man; yet I, Big Tooth, the primitive, am not a man. Somewhere, and by straight line of descent, these two parties to my dual personality were connected. Were the

Folk, before their destruction, in the process of becoming men? And did I and mine carry through this process? On the other hand, may not some descendant of mine have gone in to the Fire People and become one of them? I do not know. There is no way of learning. (18: 3)

Darwin's theory of descent with modification has raised such issues but has not provided absolute answers to these questions.

As always in the writing of London the lifelong socialist, however, it is environment rather than heredity that proves to be the really crucial factor. It is not *any* child of Big Tooth's that could transmit his memories, but only one born in particular circumstances. Early in the narrative we are assured—on the authority of a college professor—that the "racial memory" of the falling dream arose because "a terrible fall . . . was productive of shock. Such shock was productive of molecular changes in the cerebral cells. These molecular changes were transmitted to the cerebral cells of progeny, became, in short, racial memories" (2: 1). This is, essentially, straightforward Lamarckism: a child born after such an event will inherit the altered metabolism and genetic makeup of the affected parent, while one born before will not.

This seems to be the explanation for the narrator's otherwise apparently puzzling assumption that he himself must be descended from a putative child born *after* the migration rather than the definite one to whom we have already been introduced, who had been born before it: "[t]he Swift One and I managed to bring up one child, a boy—at least we managed to bring him along for several years. But I am quite confident he could never have survived that terrible climate" (18: 2). The phrasing here is evasive: the child would, we are told, certainly have died if they had stayed, and even though they didn't, we might nevertheless be led to assume that his lifespan was limited to the "several years" mentioned. In any case, no further descendance is envisaged for him, for the narrator explicitly says of the cave where they settled after their final migration, "[h]ere the Swift One and I lived and reared our family. . . . And here must have been born the child that inherited the stuff of my dreams, that had moulded into its being all the impressions of my life—or of the life of Big Tooth, rather, who is my other-self, and not my real self" (18: 3).

In short, even though the narrator cannot actually know that there ever was a later child, he prefers to believe in one rather than to imagine his earlier-born son, whom he has already in effect written off, as a link in the chain of his own later ancestry. In part this may be, as I suggested earlier, traceable back to Lamarckian ideas about the possibility of the transmission of acquired characteristics to offspring—only a child born after the migration could have transmitted to its own subsequent offspring any memories of that migration. But there seem also to be other forces at work. Throughout the narrative, the narrator has consistently pointed up the primitivism and lack of initiative of the Folk with whom Big Tooth allies himself and of whom, we suppose (though we can never be quite sure of this), he is ethnically a part. In one way, this can be fairly obviously related to the desire to produce an effect of deliberate contrast with the savage racism that so often characterized British imperialist co-options of evolutionary theory. For Haggard, the Zulus, though heroic, are developmentally on a par with the ancient Greeks; they are living anachronisms who must adapt or die—with their ability to do the former in considerable doubt since in 1864 the British Anthropological Society had declared that black children do not develop beyond the age of twelve. As Lyn Pykett remarks, "study of 'primitive' cultures proved extremely useful to the European domination of the 'dark races' in the Age of Empire" (1995, 27). Here, though, the already ideologically charged term "Folk" evokes no sense of patriotism or exclusivity, but indeed becomes virtually synonymous with idiocy: "the Folk in that day had a vocabulary of thirty or forty sounds" (4: 1), and "[w]e were ever short-sighted, we Folk" (11: 1).

Indeed it seems ultimately that Big Tooth's own progeny may survive essentially because it is also the child of the Swift One, who, he thinks, "may have been related to the Fire People" (10: 3). For his own kind, he is not only not triumphalist, he envisages no future at all. Unlike the Haggardian sense that those who are masters have always been masters and have a destiny to civilize, London's Folk are the accidental victims of colonization rather than its instigators, perhaps reflecting American resentment at their own past history as a colony. Moreover, the suggestive similarities between the Folk and Native Americans[4] touch on sensitive territory (there are, for instance, similar practices of nomenclature, and a similar pattern of suffering at the hands of technologically more advanced incomers). This comparison might well have led London to wish to present the differences between peoples in terms less confident than the imperialist adventurer Haggard, who characterized them as innate and ineradicable differences in capacity and destiny. It is true that White Fang thinks white men are a superior race to Indians (1990, 209) and that Alfred Kazin, not without reason, calls London himself "a prototype of the violence-worshiping Fascist intellectual if ever there was one in America" (1942, 111); however, Stoddard Martin argues that while "London belongs to that school which, following the theories of Darwin and Spencer, believed in an evolutionary hierarchy of races," he "was by no means so racially motivated that he would always portray his Anglo-Saxons as heroes and others as inferior villains. . . . Numerous examples from the Klondike and Hawaiian tales show London casting Indians or islanders in sympathetic roles" (1983, 41 and 46).

I think there is also another and more important reason for the mystification of the line of descent. For London, identity never exists in isolation but, as he often averred, is shaped by environment as much as heredity. Both Buck and White Fang change only because of those whom they encounter; had Buck never been stolen, or White Fang never met Weedon Scott, their behavior would have remained unaltered. In a crucial sense, then, Big Tooth's child is also the collective offspring of all the various individuals and tribes who have shaped Big Tooth's sense of his own identity. To the extent that environment thus is heredity, individual heredity is unimportant. Big Tooth's son is the child of the time, just as whiteness, in London's imaginary, is ultimately comprehensible only in terms of redness.

And this in turn takes us back to what seems to me to be the ultimate question about London's evolutionary fiction, the extent to which it is not only all men who influence an individual man's identity, but all animals. Far more subversive than *Before Adam*'s differentiation from Haggard—which would in any case be only retrospectively apparent—is its difference from a more prestigious account of man's earlier history, the Bible. The novel's very title, with its subversive suggestion of a quasi-human identity before the creation of Adam, entirely rules out the possibility of an accurate Biblical account of the origins of humanity. It is true that there are, as in so much British writing influenced by theories of evolution, occasional echoes of Milton who, along with Darwin, had been one of the two authors who had formed London's staple reading in the Klondike. For example, Big Tooth's mother, like Eve, "wore no clothes—only her natural hair" (3: 2) and he himself, like Adam, longs for the companionship of another human (2: 1), which is eventually granted in his marriage with the Swift One. But his account of his own origins is resolutely materialistic: "some strains of germplasm carry an excessive freightage of memories—are, to be scientific, more atavistic than other strains; and such a strain is mine" (2: 2). And the epigraph to chapter 1 is equally uncompromising in its insistence not only on simian but, ultimately, on marine ancestry: "These are our ancestors, and their history is our history. Remember that as surely as we one day swung down out of the trees and walked upright, just as surely, on a far earlier day, did we crawl up out of the sea and achieve our first adventure on land."

Here is what might well at first appear the darkest and most dangerous area of London's text, the implication that made his dog stories so much safer ideological territory, like Darwin's decision to describe the breeding of pigeons rather than people in *The Origin of Species*. The idea of the chain of descent touches not only on the question of human origins, and the extent of their continuity with other animal life, but the related and far more frightening one of the eventual direction of the human race. In *Before*

Adam, the question is implicitly answered by the bitter irony of the narrator, the only nugatory remnant of the Judaeo-Christian heritage, with his propensity to inexplicable and apparently unwarranted guilt, which prevents him from revealing his dreams to his parents: "I was afraid to tell. I do not know why, except that I had a feeling of guilt, though I knew no better of what I was guilty" (3: 5). Ultimately, then, even if man has progressed, it may only have been in the direction of a problematic and unnecessary complication that has belittled and bedeviled as much as it has enriched him. This, though, is where London's theories of race and speciation offer hope. If a man has listened to the voices within him and still has access to both civilized and savage modes of being, he can, like Buck in *The Call of the Wild* and the narrator in his dreams, always change back again. This is possible especially if, like Big Tooth and the heroes of the Northland stories, he cements his new-chosen identity by miscegenation. For London, who liked his own wife to call him Wolf, the man who remains in touch with both redness and whiteness will always retain something of the dual potential of the animal that can choose whether to be dog or wolf.

Notes

1. On the relation between London and Haggard, see also Gair 1997, 53.

2. Quotations from *Before Adam* (2000) are from the version available on the internet at http://sansite.berkeley.edu/London/Writings/BeforeAdam/chapter1. html. Each chapter has an appropriate variation of suffix, which provides a separate link for each of the eighteen chapters. In the interest of clarity, I therefore include only chapter and page numbers in citations within the text.

3. He had, it seems, changed his mind on this by the time he published *The Star Rover* in 1915.

4. For comment on this similarity and on London's sympathy with the Folk, see for instance Crow 1996, 50.

References

Auerbach, Jonathan. 1996. *Male Call: Becoming Jack London*. Durham, N.C.: Duke University Press.

Conan Doyle, Arthur. 1996. *The Hound of the Baskervilles*. Harmondsworth, Eng.: Penguin.

Crow, Charles L. 1996. "Ishi and Jack London's Primitives." In *Rereading Jack London*, edited by Leonard Cassuto and Jeanne Campbell Reesman. Stanford, Calif.: Stanford University Press.

Foner, Philip S. 1947. *Jack London: American Rebel*. New York: The Citadel Press.

Gair, Christopher. 1997. *Complicity and Resistance in Jack London's Novels*. Lampeter: The Edwin Mellen Press.

Geismar, Maxwell. 1954. *Rebels and Ancestors: The American Novel, 1890–1915*. London: W. H. Allen.

Haggard, H. Rider. [1927] 1971. *Allan and the Ice-Gods*. Reprint, London: Hutchinson.

Kazin, Alfred. 1942. *On Native Grounds: An Interpretation of Modern American Prose Literature*. New York: Harcourt Brace.

Labor, Earle. 1974. *Jack London*. New York: Twayne.

London, Jack. 1990. *The Call of the Wild, White Fang and Other Stories*. Edited by Earle Labor and Robert C. Leitz, III. Oxford: Oxford University Press.

———. *Before Adam*. http://sunsite.berkeley.edu/London/Writings/BeforeAdam. Accessed 15 June 2000.

Martin, Stoddard. 1983. *California Writers*. Basingstoke, Eng.: Macmillan.

Pykett, Lyn. 1995. *Engendering Fictions: The English Novel in the Early Twentieth Century*. London: Edward Arnold.

LAWRENCE I. BERKOVE

Jack London and Evolution:
From Spencer to Huxley

Among the many intellectual influences on Jack London, none is so central and profound as that of Darwin. As early as high school, London read
Darwin's *On the Origin of Species* and Herbert Spencer's Darwin-influenced
First Principles,[1] strong reading for one of his age and destined to leave a
lasting impression on his mind. A copy of the *Origin of Species* was one of the
few books London had with him in the Yukon,[2] and Darwin is mentioned
a number of times in his letters—always favorably. Scholars agree unani-
mously that Darwin was a major influence on London, most particularly
as regards the idea of evolution. This is interesting and important information as a starting point, but it is insufficient by itself to explain London's
ideas because his attitude toward evolution was not static. In some essential
respects it was shaped not so much by Darwin himself as by more popular
advocates of evolution, and over his short career it evolved in surprising but
significant ways.

There is more to Darwin's theory of evolution than the notion that mor-
phological changes occur in living organisms, developing from primitive to
more advanced and specialized forms. It maintains that evolution by natural selection is a process that develops by random changes. Therefore, it is
not only undirected, but it is also mechanical, indifferent, and remorseless. It
favors the species over the individual. It is often summed up by the phrase,
"survival of the fittest," which was added by Darwin to later editions of *Origin*

From *American Literary Realism* 36, no. 3 (Spring 2004): 243–55. Copyright © 2004 by the
University of Illinois Press.

127

of Species.[3] (His original term, which is probably more accurate, is "struggle for existence.") It was practically impossible in London's time (and it still is) to claim to accept evolution and not have an opinion on the idea behind the phrase "survival of the fittest." But a major problem with the phrase is that it fuses physical survival with some larger conception of good. Is this what Darwin meant? Is that what Nature, God, or the Life Force intended? The word "fittest," moreover, does not have a clear definition, for what is "fit" in, one situation may be unfit in another. Therefore, insofar as survival is a matter of chance rather than contest, "fittest" can have only an empirical and not an ethical meaning. This potentially important shortcoming of the phrase must be contemplated. Given that London, like most other writers, was concerned about individuals and character, it is hard to imagine why, even though he accepted Darwinism, he would be enthusiastic about a system which was not concerned about individuals and treated them all with equal indifference as expendable. The evidence leads, I believe, to the conclusion that while London was never comfortable with evolution's amoral aspects, and became less so over the years, he found a guide to reconcile his belief in Darwinism with his conviction that individuals and morality were important.[4]

London would not have been the first Darwinian to have scruples about the attractiveness of evolution. The first, in fact, was Charles Darwin himself. In a letter he wrote to the botanist J. D. Hooker on 13 July 1856, three years before *Origin of Species* was published, Darwin wrote "What a book a Devil's chaplain might write on the clumsy, wasteful, blundering low & horridly cruel works of nature!"[5] Darwin based his theory of evolution on careful, detailed, and objective observations rather than on his own ethical preferences, so when he wrote to Hooker he understood from evidence what his grandfather Erasmus Darwin had conceived in his 1803 poem "The Temple of Nature":

> Air, earth, and ocean, to astonish'd day
> One scene of blood, one mighty tomb display!
> From Hunger's arm the shafts of Death are hurl'd,
> And one great Slaughter-house the warring world![6]

Similarly, in his poem "In Memoriam" (1850) Tennyson contemplated "Nature, red in tooth and claw." But Darwin's horror at the unethical process he saw emerging from his data was not restricted to the predatory characteristics of the macro-natural world; he was also shocked by the "clumsy, wasteful, blundering low" mechanistic operation of evolution. What is ultimately so shocking about mechanistic operation was clarified by Daniel Dennett, who defined the process of evolution as a *mindless* and *purposeless* algorithmic process operating at the cellular level.

Here, then, is Darwin's dangerous idea: the algorithmic level is the level that best accounts for the speed of the antelope, the wing of the eagle, the shape of the orchid, the diversity of species, and all the other occasions for wonder in the world of nature. It is hard to believe that something as mindless and mechanical as an algorithm could produce such wonderful things. No matter how impressive the products of an algorithm, the underlying process consists of nothing but a set of individually mindless steps succeeding each other without the help of any intelligent supervision; they are "automatic" by definition: the workings of an automaton. They feed on each other, or on blind chance—coin-flips, if you like—and on nothing else.[7]

This characterization underscores the lack of purpose or direction in the feature of *randomness* in the theory of evolution; it has no brief with the notion of "survival of the fittest." Dennett's characterization, of course, is interpretive and may not be entirely valid, as modern Darwinism has different camps within it, not all in agreement with Dennett or each other.

But even in Darwin's time, as well as in later years, there were opposing camps among his advocates. The two most important for their relevance to London were those of Herbert Spencer and Thomas Huxley.[8] Spencer was the more popular of the two; he wrote for a broad and popular audience, and with the intention of making the ideas he advocated accessible to the public; his works were consequently more widely influential. It was he who coined the phrase that Darwin subsequently adopted and incorporated into later editions of *Origin of Species* "survival of the fittest." Spencer saw in evolution a harsh but ultimately salutary and therefore ethical process working for progress. Competition was good because it weeded out the inferior and improved the breed, and, he maintained, it operated in the domains of ideas and society as well as that of living organisms. This teleological aspect of evolution was not part of Darwin's theory but, as Richard Hofstadter points out, it was inferred by Spencer and other contemporary conservative thinkers and subsequently retrofitted on Darwinism.[9]

Huxley, however, a scientist in his own right, was the deeper thinker. He agreed with Darwin not just because his argument was persuasive in the way that it deductively accounted for evidence, but also because Huxley understood that the evidence with which he was personally familiar corroborated the theory of evolution. His inductive habit of mind compelled him to deal with details, even inconvenient ones, and not sweep them under the carpet of broadly valid general ideas. Spencer's phrase "survival of the fittest," as it applied to human society, was a sorely troubling detail for Huxley, and he finally openly disagreed with it in a series of papers he presented in the 1890s. The most famous of these was "Evolution and Ethics," the 1893 Romanes lecture at Oxford.

The culmination of years of reflection and study, and taking Buddhist and Greek as well as biblical thought into account along with scientific progress, the lecture judged nature as amoral and therefore unfitted to be a moral guide for humans. After explicitly dismissing social Darwinism as a "fallacy,"[10] Huxley moved to the crux of his argument: "Social progress means a checking of the cosmic process at every step and the substitution for it of another, which may be called the ethical process; the end of which is not the survival of those who may happen to be the fittest, in respect of the whole of the conditions which obtain, but of those who are ethically the best" (81). He then restates this point in a way impossible to misinterpret: "Let us understand, once for all, that the ethical progress of society depends, not on imitating the cosmic process [of evolution], still less in running away from it, but in combating it" (83).

To elaborate his position in greater detail, Huxley followed the lecture with another paper, "Prolegomena" (1894), in which he likened human civilization to a tended garden established in the wilderness, and he frankly opposed the "horticultural process" to the "cosmic process" in the garden's deliberately "creating artificial conditions of life, better adapted to the cultivated plants than are the conditions of the state of nature" (33). Huxley did not deceive himself that the horticultural process would eventually tame the cosmic process. On the contrary, he accepted not only that frustrating natural evolutionary developments would take place within the garden but also that the contest between the "State of Nature" and the "State of Art of an organized polity" would continue until the State of Nature eventually prevailed (45). Without, therefore, being able to comfort humanity with the vision of an ultimately victorious battle, Huxley nevertheless insisted that ethics was the way the human race should proceed, and that it should be on perpetual guard against following theories of perfection (including, by implication, Spencer's, for Spencer believed that perfection was the inevitable end of humanity and society), all of which would be misleading "illusions."

London quickly grasped and found common ground with Huxley's argument, but as was his wont he tested it cautiously and with deliberation. Without denigrating let alone abandoning Spencer,[11] London henceforth included Huxley as well as Darwin among his most influential teachers. From then on, although Spencer's influence on London is more obvious, the influence of Huxley on him grew and, as the record will show, soon became more profound, at least as regards evolution. "Evolution and Ethics" occasioned some published disagreements between Huxley and Spencer that were widely circulated. It was a famous dispute, and London was not only aware of it but admired it for the vigor and life of its intellectual battle. In a letter in March 1900 to Cloudsley Johns, he urged Johns to "[c]ompare the controversy of men like Spencer and Huxley, etc., etc., to the ordinary newspaper controversies between correspondents" (*Letters* I, 165). London's admiration arose from his realization that Spencer and Huxley were debating grand ideas rather than pettily sniping at personalities or ephemeral political positions.

At the very least, therefore, London was aware of the ethical difficulties inherent in extrapolating Darwinian evolution beyond biology, and he did not quickly resolve them in his own mind.[12] Throughout his fiction one can frequently recognize scenarios in which they occur, but he seems to seesaw back and forth between the Spencerian and Huxleyan positions. However, what appears in his oeuvre to be outright contradiction or, more charitably, indecision, is instead his typical pattern of trial-and-error growth. It is necessary to realize that although London lived only forty years, his philosophy was continuously, rapidly, and impressively developing and that as he assimilated and digested ideas a certain number of false starts inevitably resulted. Rather than expecting him to have from the first permanent views on every topic he broached in his literature, it is more realistic to acknowledge that his method of progressing toward final positions involved second thoughts.[13] In later works, he often revisited and sometimes revised or reversed ideas that had been clearly advocated in earlier ones, and might even have been stated forcefully. Regrettably, London's life ended before he achieved a fully mature philosophy, so it is necessary to make inferences about what it was likely to have been. It is possible to do this because, given his basic intellectual honesty and broad humanitarianism, and substantial evidence of development in his work, a fair sense of his direction can often be inferentially discerned.[14] This is the case with his Darwinian views, and a brief overview of a chronological sampling of London's works of fiction will demonstrate where, when, and how his departures from simple notions of Darwinian evolution took place.

The underestimated 1900 story, "A Relic of the Pliocene," is as good a place as any to begin. The first of two stories dealing with the Arctic adventurer Thomas Stevens, it relates "an unparalleled event in history, namely, the destruction of the oldest breed of animal on earth, and the youngest."[15] The story narrates how Stevens, enraged when a prehistoric mammoth blundered into his Arctic camp one night and inadvertently squashed to death the entire litter of a new breed of dogs he was raising, tracked, trapped, and eventually killed the mammoth with a hand axe, the only weapon he had left. Although on its surface level "A Relic" is a humorous tall tale, on a deeper level it treats tentatively two aspects of Darwinian theory: extinction of species and survival of the fittest. While Stevens may seem heroic for killing a mammoth

single-handedly, even in the early twentieth century the extinction of a species would not have been universally regarded as praiseworthy. The real mammoth, of course, was killed off in prehistoric days, and human hunters armed
with hand axes probably played a role in its extinction. This is an example of
what Darwin first called "struggle for existence," before he later replaced it
with Spencer's less accurate and more loaded phrase. No matter which phrase
we use, however, the mammoth did succumb to the attacks of a predator more
able, more fit, than it. The destruction of the new breed of dogs, however, was
a random event. The breed was not given the opportunity to prove its fitness
for survival. The matching of the two separate extinctions in the same story
illustrates two separate ideas in Darwinian theory, the struggle for existence
and the randomness of evolutionary agency, but the inclusion of the second
extinction also implies ironically that "survival of the fittest" is insufficient by
itself to account for the world we know.

"A Hyperborean Stew" (1901) continues London's process of subtly
undercutting the protagonist Thomas Stevens. In this second story, Stevens
and his Indian companion Moosu are saved from starvation when they blun-
der upon the Indian village of Tatterat on the Arctic Sea. Allotted a shack and
some food, Stevens and Moosu soon begin to repay the Tatterats' humanity
by trading off shots from a bottle of "painkiller" that was their only possession for flour, sugar, and molasses. From these items they ferment and brew
"hooch," and then trade the homemade liquor, which the Indians soon crave,
for everything the Indians own. At first Stevens and Moosu both looked
down together upon the Tatterats as primitive and inferior. But when Moosu
plans to impose his religious notions on Tatterat, conceives the idea that he
is the equal of Stevens, and then calls him "brother," Stevens resents the pre-
sumption. As soon as he recognizes that Moosu "was working out in his
own way an evolution of primitive society," that he bad ingeniously "evolved
a system of ecclesiastical taxation" (I, 507), and is now his competitor for
ruler of Tatterat, Stevens maliciously and successfully arranges to overthrow
Moosu and return him to his role as subordinate to a white man. London's
use of the term "evolution" alerts us that a speeded-up replay of "survival of
the fittest" is underway in the story. The Tatterats become the victims of the
two schemers who use the worst vices of Western "culture"—materialism,
drunkenness, and gambling—to debauch and impoverish them, and then
Stevens uses his greater knowledge to trick and bring down Moosu. As the
first tale is a criticism of "survival of the fittest," so is the second tale a parody
of Social Darwinism. Stevens and Moosu are more "fit" only in being so morally unscrupulous and ungrateful that they beggar the people who saved their
lives. And then Stevens proves himself to be more "fit" than Moosu by his
greater cunning and viciousness.[16]

The influence of Darwin is readily apparent in both stories, but from their irony it is also clear that London must be following Huxley's position rather than Spencer's. Spencer considered the extinction of inferior races a necessary part—perhaps even a duty—of progress, whereas Huxley regarded this sort of activity as savage and brutal rather than progressive. London's anti-Spencerian stance in these stories is not isolated. He continues his satire of social Darwinism in other stories of both the Arctic and the South Seas, e.g. "The Inevitable White Man" (1908), where white men prove their "fitness" not by progressive ideas of civilization and morality but by superior vice, ruthlessness, and killing power.

"The Law of Life" (1901), published after "A Relic" but before "A Hyperborean Stew," ambivalently addresses the Spencer–Huxley split as a dilemma. The story of course supports Darwin; the survival of an Indian band is aided by the willingness of the protagonist Koskoosh to sacrifice his life for it. He is old, weak, and palsied, knows himself to be a drag on his tribe, and prepares to be left for the wolves, just like an old moose he remembered whose best days were past. He assents to the "justice" of "the law of all flesh." "Nature was not kindly to the flesh. She had no concern for that concrete thing called the individual. Her interest lay in the species, the race" (I, 446–47). Before leaving Koskoosh alone in the wilderness, his son makes one last gesture of concern for him that Koskoosh paternally refuses. Later, as the wolves close in, "Koskoosh dropped his head wearily upon his knees and submitted. What did it matter after all? Was it not the law of life?" (450).

From a Spencerian perspective, Koskoosh was no longer fit for survival and the progress of the whole band required him to be left behind. But from a Huxleyan perspective, perhaps not the decision but certainly the analogy of Koskoosh with an old moose was faulty. Koskoosh was a human being and human beings, to exemplify humanity, must combat the mandates of nature. In this case, there seems to be no practical alternative to the sacrifice of Koskoosh, but by developing sympathy for Koskoosh and admiration for his son's gesture of tenderness, London appears to have recognized that while acceding to the Spencerian position might be necessary for physical survival in extreme individual cases, imitation of nature is not generally an ethically desirable course of action by which the humanity of our race progresses.

The novel *Before Adam* (1907) repeats London's building of sympathy for "non-progressive" people, in this case a doomed race of prehistoric protohominids called "the Folk." They are hunted to extinction by another race of protohominids called "the Fire People," who are slightly more "modern" in appearance, have learned how to make fire and use bows and arrows, and are very predatory. If London had been Spencerian, he would have favored the more advanced race, but instead he favored the simpler and gentler Folk. As we will see, that may have been a fateful decision.

The novel additionally makes use of another Darwinian idea, the less well-known one of "reversion," which Darwin described as the atavistic reappearance of a hereditary characteristic that has "been lost for many, perhaps for hundreds of generations."[17] The narrator of *Before Adam* is a modern American who by his own admission is "a freak of heredity, an atavistic nightmare."[18] He holds within himself an "other-personality," an ancestral "other-self" who carries a racial memory of an earlier existence as a member of the Folk, just as one of the Folk held within him a dim memory of an earlier existence as a rodent-like creature. When the narrator goes to college and studies evolution, he suddenly realizes that it gave the "key gave the explanation, gave sanity to the pranks of this atavistic brain of mine" (21). He finds that there is a rational explanation for his "prehistoric memories," and the rest of the book tells the story, from the embedded memory and perspective of a remote ancestor, of his ancestral people and how they lived and perished, victims of the murderous Fire People. Before that happens, however, his earlier self falls in love with a lone orphan woman, apparently related to the Fire People tribe, and they have a child, presumably less "advanced" than she but more than he, who survives to pass on to future generations the "germplasm" that bears memories of former existences within it, just as it bears instinct, which the narrator defines as "merely a habit that is stamped into the stuff of our heredity" (14). No less a modern Darwinian than Loren Eiseley was so deeply moved by this novel that he wrote an epilogue for it in which he confesses that he is not sure he is "satisfied about the inevitable victory of the Fire People" and suggests that "the more perceptive among us" find that "[w]e are, for all our modern skins, the lost, eternally lost, but still safe-hidden remnant of the Folk" (251). The novel is a fantasy that stretches but does not quite break Darwinian ideas, and it strongly grounds London on the Huxleyan side of the controversy, for ethics against "survival of the fittest." That, in turn, helps explain how and why a Darwinian London sided with the socialists against the captains of industry, for in the early twentieth century socialism was considered by social Darwinism to be anti-progressive.

The theme of reversion in the novel also illuminates a good deal of London's fiction and specifically explains at least two later short stories, "When the World Was Young" (1910) and "The Captain of the Susan Drew" (1912), whose protagonists both revert to an atavistic level beneath their civilized veneers. In both of these stories, however, the atavistic qualities that come to the fore are the "manly" ones of courage, assertiveness, physical aggressiveness, and leadership—the opposite of the gentler qualities of the Folk. Here again we find London in a "second thoughts" mode, looking with fresh eyes at positions that he had earlier advocated or rejected. In the first story the atavistic character uses his primitive ferocity to save the woman he loves from physical danger, and in the second the atavistic and brutal Captain Bill Decker replaces the effete gentleman capitalist Seth Gifford when the atavism is needed to help the man survive in a brutal environment. The story also resembles *The Sea-Wolf* (1904) enough to suggest that London might have been having second thoughts about his earlier denunciation of the Nietzschean Wolf Larsen, and that London might have contemplated some balance point between effete ineffectuality and brutal ruthlessness that would serve the human race better than either extreme.[19] Perhaps the character David Grief, the hero of the eight related tales collected in the book *Son of the Sun* (1912), evolved out of that problem, for Grief is best described as a Nietzschean devoted to fair play and ethical behavior.[20]

Some indication of the fascinating sifting and weighing that must have been going on in London's mind at this time can be gathered from the variety of alternatives he was considering. He returned, for example, to Spencer's social Darwinism and gave it another try in the shallow and racist potboiler novel *Adventure* (1911), written between the two aforementioned stories about atavistic return to more violent personalities.[21] In this novel, two whites, one of them the British manager of a South Seas plantation and the other a young American adventuress, quell by their superior wit and grit the insurrection caused by a cunning, ruthless, and ungrateful native and restore white domination. The characters are stereotypical, the plot is thin and predictable romance, and the theme is Anglo-Saxon superiority. But in the apocalyptic short novel *The Scarlet Place* (1912), written a year later, London reverses himself again on social Darwinism and racism when he returns to his interest in the meaning of atavism in the novella's contemplation of the near extinction of the human race by a fast-acting and untreatable plague.

Among the few random survivors are James Howard Smith, a professor at the University of California; Vesta Van Warden, the young and beautiful wife of a powerful industrialist; and Bill, her chauffeur. Their social power roles are reversed when their environment changes. The brutal chauffeur is now more "fit" than the cultured professor. He takes Vesta as his wife and becomes the founder of a tribe. As the story opens in a California that has reverted to wilderness, Smith is now known as Granser and is attended by three of Bill's grandsons, Edwin, Hoo-Hoo, and Hare-Lip. All three are uneducated and little better than savages. Edwin is the brightest, but also the most dangerous in his ambitions of violent control of others. As Granser tells them the story of how the Scarlet Plague destroyed society and civilization he confesses to what amounts to a lethal indictment against social Darwinism: "In the midst of our civilization, down in our slums and labor-ghettos, we had bred a race of barbarians, of savages; and now, in the time of our calamity, they turned upon us like the wild beasts they were and destroyed us. And they destroyed themselves as well."[22] What London understood when he wrote that passage is that there never was, is not, nor ever will be a race of superior "fittest" beings. Apart from the fact that "fitness" is always relative to variable and random external conditions, and that Darwinian thought denies perfection because evolution is, by definition, a state of constant change that is forever adapting to those varying external conditions, Granser's confession also exposes the pattern that the most advanced civilizations have always had, and probably always will have: an underclass of relative barbarians ("they") and an underclass of more talented and affluent leaders ("us") that exploits and misuses fellow human beings from the underclass. Spencer's social Darwinism, aiming at creating a superior breed, is here exposed as an illusion that leads to a dead end. London foresaw that any human society will always have strata of civilized development within it and the top level will only be a veneer of culture over the larger and lower ones of basically savage traits.[23] The race, he concluded, has not evolved far in its history. In a crisis, and not much of a crisis, most of us will readily revert to our violent prototypes, the Fire People.

London continues this pessimism in "The Red One" (1916), his brilliant and powerful "second thought" about *Adventure*, but in this remarkable story he finds one last, faint Darwinian hope in the pre Jungian themes which surface quite early in his career. Although the main character Bassett turns out to be little better than a savage himself, more dangerous because of his education and deadly technology than the primitive tribesmen, he at least recognizes in the medicine man Ngurn the seeds of ethics and, consequently, some hope for the race.[24] Judging from the specifically Jungian themes that dominate the excellent stories of his final months of life, London nursed this flickering hope into a flame. If Jungian archetypes and patterns are universally present in the human race, he seems to have reasoned, it can be argued that nature selected them for their survival value. London's last few—and obviously Jungian—stories dealing with the integration of shadow characteristics therefore result in individual human beings who besides being "fit" have evolved ethically.

Given that London's life was tragically short—he died in 1916 at age forty, probably of a stroke and heart attack resulting from uremic poisoning—any study of the evolution of his ideas must always remain somewhat conjectural. Though he died at the very height of his powers, he was in the midst of the process of reviewing and revising his earlier ideas. Those revisions, motivated by an honest acceptance of fact, all had the same direction: an increasingly broad humanitarianism. In this light, the arguments of

Huxley appear to have made a profound impression on London, increasingly replacing Spencerian positions and supplying London with the intellectual means to enable his commitment to ethics to co-exist with his conviction that Darwin's theory of evolution was correct. Following Huxley, London simultaneously believed in evolution yet trusted that however it worked out the obligation of human beings to cultivate individual ethics and pursue the goal of ethical civilization was paramount.

NOTES

1. Earle Labor and Jeanne Campbell Reesman, *Jack London*, rev. ed. (New York: Twayne, 1994), p. 12.

2. *The Letters of Jack London*, ed. Earle Labor, Robert C. Leitz, III, and I. Milo Shepard (Stanford: Stanford Univ. Press, 1993), I, 165n7. Subsequent references cited parenthetically.

3. Darwin was persuaded by his fellow scientist, Alfred Russel Wallace, to adopt the phrase. See Darwin's letter to Wallace, 5 July 1866, in *The Life and Letters of Charles Darwin*, ed. Francis Darwin (New York: Basic Books, 1959), II, 229–30. Wallace had independently approximated Darwin's theory but, according to Adrian Desmond and James Moore, *Darwin* (London: Penguin, 1991), p. 468, Wallace's "theory differed from Darwin's. Wallace's idea of selection was the environment eliminating the unfit, rather than a cut-throat competition among individuals." Wallace, in other words, believed that natural law was progressive in its ends, whereas Darwin restricted himself to describing the operation of natural selection without speculating on its purpose.

4. In maintaining the importance to London of individuals, I am unable to go as far as Howard Horowitz in "Primordial Stories: London and the Immateriality of Evolution," *Western Humanities Review*, 50 (Winter/Spring 1997), 337–43, which argues, in effect, an extreme and radical individualism in London that dismisses the ethical complexities of evolution as "immaterial" because "the impulse to survive" is the supreme mandate of life: "All individual effort and all cultures and all epochs are his instantiations [sic] of the same, simple and elegant law." Horowitz holds that to London, the Darwinian idea of adaptation is transformed into *individual* adaptability; i.e., the mechanism of natural selection is shifted "from accident and variation to hereditary necessity and individual transcendence of environment." It appears that Horowitz not only oversimplifies the problems raised by Spencer and addressed by Huxley and reduces issues of society, love, loyalty, and civilization to a matter of individual survival, but also has London taking such liberties with Darwin that he is ultimately "anti-evolutionary."

5. *The Correspondence of Charles Darwin* (New York: Cambridge Univ. Press, 1990), VI, 178.

6. Quoted in *The Essential Writings of Erasmus Darwin*, ed. Desmond King-Hele (London: MacGibbon & Kee, 1968), p. 93. Erasmus Darwin is often praised for his remarkable anticipation in *Zoonomia* (1794) and other works of his grandson's theory of evolution.

7. Daniel C. Dennett, *Darwin's Dangerous Idea: Evolution and the Meanings of Life* (New York: Simon & Schuster, 1995), pp. 59, 320.

8. London's relative ranking of Darwinists at an early stage of his career can be seen in his 10 August 1899 letter to Cloudsley Johns: "Spencer's *First Principles* alone, leaving out all the rest of his work, has done more for mankind, and through the ages will have done far more for mankind, than a thousand of books like *Nicholas Nickleby, Hard Cash, Book of Snobs*, and *Uncle Tom's Cabin*. Why take the enormous power for good contained in Darwin's *Origin of Species* and *Descent of Man*. Or in the work of Ruskin, Mill, Huxley, Carlyle, Ingersoll" (Letters I, 104).

9. Richard Hofstadter, *Social Darwinism in American Thought*, rev. ed. (Boston: Beacon, 1955), pp. 4–8.

10. Thomas H. Huxley, *Evolution and Ethics and Other Essays* (New York: Appleton, 1915), pp. 80–81. Subsequent references are cited parenthetically.

11. London appears to have been discriminating in his reading of Spencer, and could be lukewarm or negative toward one feature of Spencer's ideas while supporting others. For example, although he was uncomfortable with Spencer's notion of survival of the fittest, Barbara Lundquist claims that he remained an adherent of Spencer's *Philosophy of Style* and found Spencer's explanation of the first law of thermodynamics sufficiently persuasive to use it throughout *Martin Eden* (1908–09). See her "Jack London, Aesthetic Theory, and Nineteenth-Century Popular Science," *Western American Literature*, 32 (August 1997), 99–114.

12. London's difficulties with Spencerian ideas on evolution have long been noticed in London scholarship. Frances W. Kaye observed in "Jack London's Modification of Herbert Spencer," *Jack London Newsletter*, 7 (1974), 68, that "London does not quite take his Spencer straight, for the survival of the fittest leads to the wild, not to civilization." Sam Baskett in *"Martin Eden*: Jack London's 'Splendid Dream,'" *Western American Literature*, 12 (1977), 204–05, quotes Martin Eden to the effect that Spencer "unified the universe" for him, but goes on to point out that that unity is "precarious" and eventually shattered because Martin Eden subsequently finds himself in a universe of intolerably cold, abstract knowledge without personal warmth. Anthony J. Naso in "Jack London and Herbert Spencer," *Jack London Newsletter* 14, (1981), 29, concludes that "Deeply impressed as he was with Spencer, London found himself rejecting those aspects of Spencer's philosophy that went counter to his convictions that love and loyalty have a value in human relationships and that all men must unite in the effort to improve the human condition."

13. Lawrence I. Berkove, "Jack London's 'Second Thoughts': The Short Fiction of His Late Period," *Jack London: One Hundred Years a Writer*, ed. Sara S. Hobson and Jeanne Campbell Reesman (San Marino, Cal.: Huntington Library, 2002), pp. 60–76, accounts for ideological contradictions in London's short stories not as irresponsible confusion or indecision but as products of his way of revisiting and retesting competing ideas in a search for truth. Over a period of time progress can be seen in the stories toward refined ideas and consistency. It is now apparent that the same habit of mind affects his longer works as well.

14. I am aware that London continued to make biased comments about race well into his career, and that Earle Labor described him as "a bundle of contradictions in such matters." But London would be far from the first author to let himself go in personal relationships and, for a variety of possible reasons, express prejudices that he came to recognize as unworthy when he wrote "for the record." In his personal life London was no saint, but the literary record shows him making determined progress in transcending his biases and moving toward more liberal ideals.

15. *The Complete Short Stories of Jack London*, ed. Earle Labor, Robert C. Leitz III and I. Milo Shepard (Stanford: Stanford Univ. Press, 1993), I, 496. Subsequent references are noted parenthetically.

16. For a fuller discussion of these stories see Lawrence I. Berkove, "Thomas Stevens: London's Comic Agent of Evolutionary Criticism," Thalia, 12, i–ii (1992), 61–68.

17. Charles Darwin, *On the Origin of Species: A Facsimile of the First Edition* (Cambridge: Harvard Univ. Press, 1964), pp. 160ff.

18. London, *Before Adam* (1906; rpt. Lincoln: Univ. of Nebraska Press, 2000), p. 20. Subsequent references are noted parenthetically.

19. See Lawrence I. Berkove, "The Captain of the Susan Drew: The Reworking of *The Sea-Wolf*," Thalia, 17, i–ii (1997), 61–68.

20. For further elaboration of this point, see the introduction by Thomas R. Tietze and Gary J. Riedl to *A Son of the Sun* (Norman: Univ. of Oklahoma Press, 2001), esp. pp. xviii–xxv.

21. Clarice Stasz discusses the social Darwinian background of the novel in "Social Darwinism, Gender, and Humor in *Adventure*," *Rereading Jack London*, ed. Leonard Cassuto and Jeanne Campbell Reesman (Stanford: Stanford Univ. Press, 1986), pp. 130–40, 259–60.

22. London, *The Scarlet Plague* (1912; rpt. New York: Arno, 1975), pp. 106–06.

23. The savage implications of social Darwinism, and London's near-disenchantment with it, can be seen even in his novel *The Mutiny of the Elsinore* (1913; rpt. New York: Arcadia, 1950), published a year after *The Scarlet Plague*. There is evidence in the novel that its typical Anglo-Saxon protagonist Pathurst is not necessarily its hero. Apart from his naiveté and blatant and simplistic racism, his view of things does not satisfactorily account for either events or personalities. A perceptive crewman criticizes both Pathurst's party and the mutineers. The mutineers, he charges, "are what you an' your fathers have made 'em. An' who in hell are you and your fathers? Robbers of the toil of men" (371). Even Pathurst recognizes that "we are a lot of primitive beasts, fighting bestially, slaying bestially. . . . We are all dogs—there is no getting away from it. And we, the fair-pigmented ones, by the seed of our ancestry rulers in the high places, shall remain top dog over the rest of the dogs" (348–49). Thus Pathurst acknowledges that his kind are just more cunning animals.

24. For an interpretation of this story, see Lawrence I. Berkove, "The Myth of Hope in Jack London's 'The Red One,'" *Rereading Jack London*, pp. 204–15.

Chronology

1876   Born in San Francisco on January 12, the only child of Flora Wellman. She names the child John Griffith Chaney and says his father is William Henry Chaney, whom she lived with from 1874 to 1875. On September 7, Flora marries John London, and the baby is named John Griffith London.

1891   Completes grammar school. Works in a cannery. In 1891 or 1892, he buys a sloop; raids oyster beds. Later serves as officer of California Fish Patrol.

1893   Wins first prize in San Francisco *Call*'s Best Descriptive Article Contest for "Story of a Typhoon off the Coast of Japan."

1894 or 1895   Arrested for vagrancy and serves one month in Erie County Penitentiary, New York. In 1895, resumes high school education at Oakland High School, where he writes sketches and stories for a student magazine.

1896   Joins Socialist Labor Party. Attends University of California for one semester.

1897–1898   Gold miner in Yukon Territory. John London dies in 1897.

1898 or 1899   Becomes professional writer. In 1899, publishes first story, "To the Man on Trail" in *Overland Monthly*.

1900   Publishes "An Odyssey of the North" in the *Atlantic Monthly*. Marries Bessie Maddern on April 7. First book, *The Son of the Wolf*, published.

1901	First daughter, Joan, born.
1902	Lives in London's East End ghetto for six weeks, collecting material for his sociological study *The People of the Abyss*. Second daughter, Bess, is born. First novel, *A Daughter of the Snows*, published.
1903	Separates from Bessie. *The Call of the Wild* is published and becomes instant success.
1904	War correspondent for Russo-Japanese War for Hearst syndicate. Publishes *The Sea-Wolf*.
1905	Divorces wife. Marries Charmian Kittredge. Purchases ranch in California. Lectures in the East; in 1905 or 1906, lectures in the Midwest.
1906	Lectures at Yale. Reports on San Francisco earthquake and fire for *Collier's*. Begins building his sailboat, the *Snark*. Publishes *White Fang*.
1907	Sets sail from California on the *Snark*; visits Hawaii, the Marquesas, and Tahiti.
1908	Returns home briefly aboard steamship to attend to financial affairs. Continues *Snark* trip, sailing to Samoa, Fiji Islands, New Hebrides, and the Solomons. *The Iron Heel* is published.
1909	Hospitalized in Australia for multiple tropical ailments. Abandons plans for sailing *Snark* around the world and returns to California on coal transport vessel. Publishes *Martin Eden*.
1910	Focuses on building his Beauty Ranch; begins construction of Wolf House, his mansion. Daughter Joy is born and dies.
1912	Sails for more than four months around Cape Horn aboard the *Dirigo*. Wife has a miscarriage.
1913	Wolf House is destroyed by fire. *John Barleycorn*, semiautobiographical work on alcoholism, is published.
1914	Reports on Mexican Revolution for *Collier's*.
1915	Spends several months in Hawaii for health reasons. *The Star Rover* is published.
1916	Resigns from Socialist Labor Party. Dies on November 22 in California of uremic poisoning.

Contributors

HAROLD BLOOM is Sterling Professor of the Humanities at Yale University. Educated at Cornell and Yale universities, he is the author of more than 30 books, including *Shelley's Mythmaking* (1959), *The Visionary Company* (1961), *Blake's Apocalypse* (1963), *Yeats* (1970), *The Anxiety of Influence* (1973), *A Map of Misreading* (1975), *Kabbalah and Criticism* (1975), *Agon: Toward a Theory of Revisionism* (1982), *The American Religion* (1992), *The Western Canon* (1994), *Omens of Millennium: The Gnosis of Angels, Dreams, and Resurrection* (1996), *Shakespeare: The Invention of the Human* (1998), *How to Read and Why* (2000), *Genius: A Mosaic of One Hundred Exemplary Creative Minds* (2002), *Hamlet: Poem Unlimited* (2003), *Where Shall Wisdom Be Found?* (2004), and *Jesus and Yahweh: The Names Divine* (2005). In addition, he is the author of hundreds of articles, reviews, and editorial introductions. In 1999, Professor Bloom received the American Academy of Arts and Letters' Gold Medal for Criticism. He has also received the International Prize of Catalonia, the Alfonso Reyes Prize of Mexico, and the Hans Christian Andersen Bicentennial Prize of Denmark.

DONALD PIZER is an emeritus professor of Tulane University. He has published several books on the naturalist movement, including *American Naturalism and the Jews*, *Realism and Naturalism in Nineteenth-Century American Literature*, and *Twentieth-Century American Literary Naturalism*.

SAM S. BASKETT is a professor emeritus of Michigan State University and was the first president of the Jack London Society. His publications include the Rinehart edition of *Martin Eden* and many essays on London.

143

JONATHAN AUERBACH is a professor at the University of Maryland. He has published *Male Call: Becoming Jack London* and editions of London's *Northland Tales* and *The Iron Heel*.

ANDREW J. FURER has taught at the University of Connecticut, Fordham University, and Harvard University. He is the author of articles on London, Dreiser, and other naturalist writers.

CHRISTOPHER GAIR is a senior lecturer at the University of Glasgow. He is editor of London's *South Sea Tales*. He is also the author of *The Beat Generation: A Beginner's Guide* and other titles.

JAMES A. PAPA JR. is an associate professor at the City University of New York. He has written essays on Edward Abbey, Henry David Thoreau, and Annie Dillard, as well as several book reviews.

PER SERRITSLEV PETERSEN has been an associate professor at Aarhus University in Denmark, where he also has been chairman of the English department. He has published widely, covering British and American studies, literary and cultural theory, and individual authors, including London.

LISA HOPKINS is a professor at Sheffield Hallam University, United Kingdom. She has written many texts, including *Giants of the Past: Popular Fictions and the Idea of Evolution*. She also has been coeditor of *Shakespeare*, the journal of the British Shakespeare Association.

LAWRENCE I. BERKOVE is professor emeritus at the University of Michigan, Dearborn. An authority on Ambrose Bierce, Mark Twain, Jack London, and the writers of the "Sagebrush School," he is the author of 10 books and monographs, most recently *A Prescription for Adversity: The Moral Art of Ambrose Bierce*.

Bibliography

Auerbach, Jonathan. *Male Call: Becoming Jack London*. Durham, N.C.: Duke University Press, 1996.

Baskett, Sam. "Mythic Dimensions of 'All Gold Canyon.'" *Jack London Journal* 2 (1995): 10–24.

Beauchamp, Gorman. *Jack London*. San Bernardino, Calif.: Borgo Press, 1984.

Berliner, Jonathan. "Jack London's Socialistic Social Darwinism." *American Literary Realism* 41, no. 1 (Fall 2008): 52–78.

Campbell, Donna. "Jack London's Allegorical Landscapes: *The God of His Fathers*, *The Priestly Prerogative*, and *The Valley of the Moon*." *Literature and Belief* 21, no. 1/2 (2001): 59–75.

Cassuto, Leonard, and Jeanne Campbell Reesman, ed. *Rereading Jack London*. Stanford, Calif.: Stanford University Press, 1996.

Doctorow, E. L. *Jack London, Hemingway, and the Constitution: Selected Essays, 1977–1992*. New York: Random House, 1993.

Dooley, Patrick K. "'The Strenuous Mood': William James' 'Energies in Men' and Jack London's *The Sea Wolf*." *American Literary Realism* 34, no. 1 (Fall 2001): 18–28.

Ellis, Juniper. "A 'wreckage of races' in Jack London's South Pacific." *Arizona Quarterly* 57, no. 2 (2001): 57–75.

Farrier, David. *Unsettled Narratives: The Pacific Writings of Stevenson, Ellis, Melville and London*. New York: Routledge, 2007.

Furer, Andrew J. "Jack London's New Woman: A Little Lady with a Big Stick." *Studies in American Fiction* 22, no. 2 (Autumn 1994): 185–214.

Gair, Christopher "Gender and Genre: Nature, Naturalism, and Authority in *The Sea-Wolf*." *Studies in American Fiction* 22, no. 2 (Autumn 1994): 131–47.

145

————. "London Calling: The Importance of Jack London to Contemporary Cultural Studies." *Works and Days: Essays in the Socio-Historical Dimensions of Literature and the Arts* 11 (Fall 1993): 27–43.

Gatti, Susan. "The Dark Laughter of Darrell Standing: Comedy and the Absurd in Jack London's *The Star Rover.*" *Thalia* 12, no. 1/2 (1992): 25–32.

Gatti, Susan Irvin. "Stone Hearths and Marble Babies: Jack London and the Domestic Ideal." *Jack London Journal* 3 (1996): 43–56.

Harvey, Anne-Marie. "Sons of the Sun: Making White, Middle-Class Manhood in Jack London's David Grief Stories and the *Saturday Evening Post.*" *American Studies* 39, no. 3 (1998): 37–68.

Hayes, Kevin J. "How Jack London Read Joseph Conrad." *American Literary Realism* 30, no. 2 (Winter 1998): 17–27.

Hedrick, Joan D. "London's Socialist Fiction." *Solitary Comrade: Jack London and His Work*. Chapel Hill: University of North Carolina Press, 1982.

Hodson, Sara. S., and Jeanne Campbell Reesman, ed. *Jack London: One Hundred Years a Writer*. San Marino, Calif.: Huntington Library Press, 2002.

Johnston, Carolyn. *Jack London—An American Radical?* Westport, Conn.: Greenwood Press, 1984.

Kumin, Michael. "*The Call of the Wild*: London's Seven Stages of Allegory." *Jack London Newsletter* 21, nos. 1–3 (January–December 1988): 86–98.

Labor, Earle, and Jeanne Campbell Reesman. *Jack London*. New York: Twayne Publishers: Maxwell Macmillan, 1994.

Lawlor, Mary. *Recalling the Wild: Naturalism and the Closing of the American West*. New Brunswick, N.J.: Rutgers University Press, 2000.

Lindquist, Barbara. "Jack London, Aesthetic Theory, and Nineteenth-Century Popular Science." *Western American Literature* 32, no. 2 (Summer 1997): 99–114.

Lundquist, James. *Jack London: Adventures, Ideas, and Fiction*. New York: Ungar, 1987.

Martin, Stoddard. *California Writers: Jack London, John Steinbeck, the Tough Guys*. New York: St. Martin's Press, 1983.

McClintock, James I. *Jack London's Strong Truths*. East Lansing: Michigan State University Press, 1997.

Oliveri, Vinnie. "Sex, Gender, and Death in *The Sea-Wolf.*" *Pacific Coast Philology*, 38 (2003): 99–115.

Raskin, Jonah, ed. *The Radical Jack London: Writings on War and Revolution*. Berkeley: University of California Press, 2008.

Reesman, Jeanne Campbell. *Jack London: A Study of the Short Fiction*. New York: Twayne Publishers, 1999.

———. "Jack London's New Woman in a New World: Saxon Brown Roberts' Journey into the Valley of the Moon." *American Literary Realism* 24, no. 2 (Winter 1992): 40–54.

———. "'Never Travel Alone': Naturalism, Jack London, and the White Silence." *American Literary Realism* 29, no. 2 (Winter 1997): 33–49.

Robisch, S. K. *Wolves and the Wolf Myth in American Literature.* Reno: University of Nevada Press, 2009.

Rossetti, Gina M. *Imagining the Primitive in Naturalist and Modernist Literature.* Columbia: University of Missouri Press, 2006.

Shaheen, Aaron. "The Competing Narratives of Modernity in Jack London's *The Iron Heel.*" *American Literary Realism* 41, no. 1 (2008): 35–51.

Shor, Francis. "*The Iron Heel*'s Marginal(ized) Utopia." *Extrapolation* 35, no. 3 (1994): 211–29.

Stasz, Clarice. *Jack London's Women.* Amherst: Massachusetts University Press, 2001.

Tavernier-Courbin, Jacqueline. *The Call of the Wild: A Naturalistic Romance.* New York: Twayne Publishers; Toronto: Maxwell Macmillan Canada; New York: Maxwell Macmillan International, 1994.

———. *Critical Essays on Jack London.* Boston: G. K. Hall, 1983.

Walker, Dale L., and Jeanne Campbell Reesman, ed. *No Mentor But Myself: Jack London on Writers and Writing.* Stanford, Calif.: Stanford University Press; Cambridge: Cambridge University Press, 1999.

Watson, Charles N., Jr. *The Novels of Jack London: A Reappraisal.* Madison: University of Wisconsin Press, 1983.

Williams, James. "The Composition of Jack London's Writings." *American Literary Realism* 23, no. 2 (1991): 64–86.

Williams, Tony. "Jack London and the Dialogic Imagination." *Jack London Newsletter* 21, nos. 1–3 (January–December 1988): 128–38.

Acknowledgments

Donald Pizer, "Jack London: The Problem of Form." From *Studies in the Literary Imagination* 16, no. 2 (Fall 1983): 107–15. Copyright © 1983 by Georgia State University.

Sam S. Baskett, "Sea Change in *The Sea-Wolf.*" From *American Literary Realism 1870–1910* 24, no. 2 (Winter 1992): 5–22. Copyright © 1992 by McFarland & Company.

Jonathan Auerbach, "'Congested Mails': Buck and Jack's 'Call.'" From *American Literature* 67, no. 1 (March 1995): 51–76. Copyright © 1995 by Duke University Press.

Andrew J. Furer, "'Zone-Conquerors' and 'White Devils': The Contradictions of Race in the Works of Jack London." From *Rereading Jack London*, edited by Leonard Cassuto and Jeanne Campbell Reesman. Copyright © 1996 by the Board of Trustees of Leland Stanford Junior University.

Christopher Gair, "The Wires Were Down: The Telegraph and the Cultural Self in 'To Build a Fire' and *White Fang.*" From *Complicity and Resistance in Jack London's Novels: From Naturalism to Nature.* Published by the Edwin Mellen Press. Copyright © 1997 by Christopher Gair.

James A Papa Jr., "Canvas and Steam: Historical Conflict in Jack London's *Sea-Wolf.*" From *Midwest Quarterly* 40, no. 3 (1999): 274–84. Copyright © 1999 by *Midwest Quarterly.*

149

Per Serritslev Petersen, "Jack London's Medusa of Truth." From *Philosophy and Literature* 26, no. 1 (April 2002): 43–56. Copyright © 2002 by *Philosophy and Literature*.

Lisa Hopkins, "Jack London's Evolutionary Hierarchies: Dogs, Wolves, and Men." From *Evolution and Eugenics in American Literature and Culture, 1880–1940: Essays on Ideological Conflict and Complicity*, edited and with an introduction by Lois A. Cuddy and Claire M. Roche. Published by Bucknell University Press. Copyright © 2003 by Rosemont Publishing and Printing.

Lawrence I. Berkove, "Jack London and Evolution: From Spenser to Huxley." From *American Literary Realism* 36, no. 3 (Spring 2004): 243–55. Copyright © 2004 by the University of Illinois Press.

Index

Characters in literary works are indexed by first name (if any), followed by the name of the work in parentheses